MW00790255

INTEGRITY

The Guarantee for Success

by
Frederick K.C. Price, D.D.

Faith One Publishing
Los Angeles, California

INTEGRITY
The Guarantee for Success
ISBN 1-883798-42-6
Copyright © 2000 by
Frederick K.C. Price, D.D.
PO Box 90000
Los Angeles, CA 90009

Published by Faith One Publishing
7901 South Vermont Avenue
Los Angeles, California 90044

Publisher's Cataloging-in-Publication
(Provided by Quality Books, Inc.)

Price, Frederick K.C.
    Integrity : the guarantee for success / by
Frederick K.C. Price. -- 1st ed.
    p. cm.
    ISBN: 1-883798-42-6

    1. Integrity--Religious aspects--Christianity.
    2. Success--Religious aspects--Christianity.
    3. Conduct of life. 4. Spiritual life.   I. Title.

BV4647.I55P75 2000   241.4
                 QB100-394

TABLE OF CONTENTS

INTRODUCTION

Say you are driving to work and are running about ten minutes late. You need to make up for lost time. So, since you do not see any cars ahead, you decide to do what many people do when approaching a stop sign — slow down, but fail to make a complete stop.

But just as your car enters the intersection, a young child chasing a ball darts into the crosswalk ahead. If only you had come to a full stop, you could have avoided what is now inevitable. This is one error in judgment that you will never forget. For the rest of your life you will be haunted by the fact that your disregard for a simple traffic sign cost the life of a young child. No amount of remorse can bring that child back to life.

Maybe you never run stop signs. But say you are married and one day your boss invites you to dinner after work. You sense that he or she is interested in more than just working with you. Still, rather than deal with this situation up front, you either accept the invitation or try to find some excuse to get out of going.

In either case, the door is open for trouble. You may tell yourself, *Well, one little dinner wouldn't hurt anything*, and, in fact, the dinner could go just fine. But, then again, it may not. Regardless, your spouse is going to wonder why you did not come home right after work.

If you sidestep the issue with excuses, you may avoid offending your supervisor, but only temporarily. More than likely, your boss will continue extending invitations. There you are, hoping that he or she will get the hint and stop asking, while your supervisor's anticipation is growing. There will come a time when your boss will rightfully feel as though you are stringing him or her along. Then, you will have a lot more than just feelings of rejection to handle. And what is your spouse going to think when he or she hears that you did not say no right from the start?

Things inevitably work out better when you do the right thing. Unfortunately, many people do not act on what they know to be right at the time. They are so afraid to face the issue squarely, that they fail to consider the long-term consequences. They sell themselves short by taking the path of least resistance, and wind up having to pay through the nose.

I am not suggesting that being a person of integrity is easy, or that it will not cost you something, but that the expense is much less when you pay up front. There is biblical precedence for this. The account of Daniel says that the prophet distinguished himself so much above his peers, because an "excellent spirit" was in him, that the king wanted to promote him. What exactly was this "excellent spirit" that distinguished Daniel so greatly that the king took note of him?

It was integrity. Daniel's adversaries said they would not be able to catch him in any wrongdoing unless they accused Daniel of doing what was right, but made it seem as if it was wrong. They were admitting that Daniel was a faultless man.

Daniel demonstrated his integrity by the way he responded to the plot against him. When his enemies persuaded the king to decree that no man could petition any god except the king for 30 days, what did Daniel do? He went home and continued doing as was his custom: praying and giving thanks to his God, Jehovah. Daniel even left the window of his home open for all to see. He did not allow their scheme and what it could cost him deter him from doing what he knew was right.

And it did cost Daniel something — a night in the lions' den. But in the morning, Daniel was freed, unharmed, because his God had shut the mouths of the lions. Daniel was able to endure the consequences and go on to prosper in the reign of two kings — Darius and Cyrus the Persian. Daniel ended up more than just promoted; he came out ahead of where he might have advanced otherwise. For Daniel, maintaining his relationship with God proved far more valuable than the cost of one night in the lions' den.

There are always going to be challenges in life and, more times than not, it is how we handle these challenges that determine how things turn out and, consequently, the quality of life we enjoy. Integrity will not always look like the way to go, but it pays off in the long run. Despite what others say about the need to be and do what is politically correct and socially acceptable, integrity is the key to experiencing the kind of success that is worth having.

ONE

ROLLING THROUGH STOP SIGNS

America has become a nation of lawbreakers. We make up our own laws as we go along. Somewhere along the line, we decided that a stop sign means to slow down. If you were to ask someone why they failed to stop at a stop sign, they would probably say, "But everyone does rolling stops."

The majority rules, despite what the law says; and any and everything is now considered to be all right until someone gets hurt. So, to avoid hurting someone's feelings justifies not telling him the truth, when the truth would have prevented him from an even greater degree of hurt down the line.

With these kinds of attitudes prevalent in society, it is necessary to take a look at what it means to have integrity. I have found that people have varying ideas about integrity and most do not have a lifestyle to support what they believe. I certainly do not see them acting like the prophet Daniel in the midst of their adversities. Daniel refused to allow other people to dictate how he lived his life. He did not just go along with what everyone else was doing. So, how can people possibly hope to succeed the way Daniel did if they just follow the crowd?

That is why I want to go to the same source as Daniel to find out what he knew about integrity. There is a proverb that Daniel would have been familiar with that reveals a very important aspect of integrity. It says:

The integrity of the upright will guide them, but the perversity of the unfaithful will destroy them.

You could say that Proverbs 11:3 reveals that: *The upright will be guided by their integrity.* In other words, integrity is supposed to be a guide. To what? The truth. But integrity is not, in and of itself, the truth. It is the guide to acting on the truth.

Integrity forces you to question and analyze your situation.

For example, say you see something that looks like a curtain, but you are not certain. So, you walk over to take a closer look and discover that it is a curtain. That inclination to want to know for sure, and the steps you took to find out, are your integrity at work.

Integrity is the process of discerning right from wrong and then doing what you know to be right. Say you give the cashier at the supermarket $10 to pay for $8.50 worth of groceries, but the cashier hands you back $11.50 in change. It would be wrong to pocket the extra $10. That is the truth. But it is your integrity that sees that you have been given too much change and compels you to hand it back.

So you see, integrity guides you to know what the truth is by compelling you to want to act on what is right. Without this quality, without this factor involved, you will go whichever way the wind is blowing, despite what you know to be true.

Now, you may not always agree with someone as to what is the right thing to do in a given situation, yet you could both be people of integrity. What distinguishes someone as a person of integrity is that they routinely act on what they know to be right. I need to point this out because the truth is not always immediately apparent. And oftentimes what one person calls right is wrong and what another person calls wrong is right.

In fact, determining the truth nowadays is not unlike the old saying: "Beauty is in the eye of the beholder." For instance, what is beautiful? Whatever you think is beautiful — and if enough people say it is beautiful, then it is. Likewise, the truth is often mistakenly seen as subjective and is manipulated by public opinion. This is why integrity is so important — because it causes you to always assess the situation for yourself and to then do what *you* know to be right.

This brings me to another aspect of integrity: You must be willing to make a quick change, if what you believe is right in a given situation turns out to be wrong. There is no shame in admitting that you have made a mistake. It does not mean that you lack integrity; it simply means that you made a mistake. After all, the fact that integrity is only a guide lets you know that you will have to analyze and judge things, and there are bound to be times when you will discover more information or just plain realize that you have been wrong.

Integrity demands that, if you find you have made a mistake, you do not try to excuse it on the basis that "Every-

3

one does rolling stops." Nor do you try to hide the fact. You should be the first to admit your mistake and make the correction publicly, when the situation calls for it.

Integrity is not some "one-time" deal. It is a life-long process — something you do all the time. Making the right decision and doing the right thing once or twice in your life does not make you a person of integrity. It simply made you right those times.

According to Webster's Dictionary, *integrity* means the quality or state of being of sound moral principle, uprightness, honesty and sincerity. It is a quality or a state of being. In other words, it is something that you are doing on a consistent basis, just as the proverb says.

What does it take to be a person of integrity? The word *moral* found in the definition of integrity simply means good or right in conduct or character; virtuous in sexual conduct; principles; standards or habits with respect to right or wrong in conduct; ethics. This definition brings me to two words that I believe bear explanation: *character* and *ethics.*

Character refers to moral strength, self-discipline, fortitude, or a good reputation; it is what enables you to act on what your integrity guides you to believe is right. *Ethics* is a system of moral standards or values that is the foundation for your actions. It is because of your ethics that you do what you do and why you do not do some things that you could do. Ethics is simply that by which you govern yourself.

Everyone has ethics, a value system — even the thief and the liar. Of course, the ethics of a thief or a liar should be different from yours. Nonetheless, they still have ethics;

they still have a system by which they operate. A liar has ethics about his lying. He typically justifies lying on the belief that: "Well, if I don't lie to them, they are going to lie to me. If I don't get them first, they'll get me."

Having ethics does not guarantee that you will do what is right or that you will stay out of legal trouble. If your ethics are warped, then your value judgment will be warped because you can only make value judgments based upon what is in you. So if you do not have a sound moral standard or ethics in you, you are liable to do just about anything. That is why it is not until you combine morals and character with your ethics that you become a person of integrity — a person whose faculties guide him to do what is right.

Let me ask you a question: Do you have a standard by which you govern yourself and keep your circumstances from dictating your actions? Your answer depends on your morals and character, does it not? If you lack morals or character, your ethics may, and often will, change to suit your circumstances. But if you have morals, ethics and character combined, you will stand up and say, "I do this because I choose to, because I made a commitment to do it, since it is the right thing to do. It does not matter whether anyone else is doing it. Regardless, here is where I stand." This is integrity talking.

A man of integrity takes integrity personally. He is his own person. He does not do something simply because he sees other people doing it. He follows the guide that is within him — not the crowd. He lets this guide, not his circumstances, lead him in developing his ethics. And he has such character, such intestinal fortitude and self-discipline, that he will consistently do what he knows is morally right despite the consequences. This is what it means to be a person of integrity — and it takes morals, character and ethics, which is why these are inherent in the very meaning of integrity.

Now you should be able to see why people like Daniel endure and rise above the consequences, while those who roll right through stop signs typically fall victim to their circumstances. Integrity makes all the difference in the world.

MAKING THE COMMITMENT

Having integrity means consistently acting on what you believe is right. Since everyone can benefit as Daniel did from living a life of integrity, I want to share with you the three components involved in acting on what you believe is right.

Operating with integrity is a threefold process:

Step #1. *Discerning what is right and what is wrong.*

There has to be a right and a wrong. If there is a right, there has to be a corresponding wrong and vice versa. This is very obvious point, but many miss it.

Step #2. *Acting on what you have discerned, even at great personal cost.*

Even though people discern right from wrong, they think the price tag for doing what they know is right is too high. The man or woman of integrity, however, acts on what he or she has discerned to be right, regardless. While most people will go with what is convenient (as long as it does not

7

cost them too much), the person of integrity does what he believes is right despite the cost, because his integrity means more to him than anything else. He will take action.

Step #3. *Saying openly that you are acting on your understanding of right and wrong.*

In other words, make a public declaration of where you stand. You do this so that there is no gray area, no ambiguity regarding your position. I call this making a commitment. Integrity involves a willingness to make a commitment to what you believe.

The voice of integrity says, "I don't know what you're going to do, but I know what I have to do. This is right, and this is wrong." When people try to say, "Yeah, but everyone's doing it." Integrity still says, "So? Here's where I stand." Even if others claim, "Yeah, but popular opinion is…" integrity does not change its mind. People may try to coerce you by saying, "You're going to be standing out there by yourself," but integrity points out, "Regardless, here's where *I* stand."

Since the truth does not stand alone in a vacuum — it has to be connected to something so you can see what it means — I want to give some examples of how integrity operates so that it is very clear how these three steps work together. I have found two examples in the Bible that illustrate what I have just explained.

The first example is the account of three Hebrew boys, Shadrach, Meshach, and Abed-Nego, found in the third chapter of the Book of Daniel, which begins by saying:

Nebuchadnezzar the king made an image of gold, whose height was sixty cubits and its width six cubits. He set it up in the plain of Dura, in the province of Babylon.

Allow me to point out that the king's idol stood in direct opposition to the commandment not to worship any other god but Jehovah passed-down to these three boys by their forefathers.

Then a herald cried aloud: "To you it is commanded, O peoples, nations, and languages,

"that at the time you hear the sound of the horn, flute, harp, lyre, and psaltery, in symphony with all kinds of music, you shall fall down and worship the gold image that King Nebuchadnezzar has set up;

"and whoever does not fall down and worship shall be cast immediately into the midst of a burning fiery furnace."

Now there is a price tag tied to the product. To take a stand and declare that what the king had done was wrong would cost them. They had a decision, a value judgment, to make.

So at that time, when all the people heard the sound of the horn, flute, harp, and lyre, in symphony with all kinds of music, all the people, nations, and languages fell down and worshipped the gold image which King Nebuchadnezzar had set up.

Everyone else was falling down and worshipping the image. No one would have noticed if the three boys had gone along and fell down to worship it as well. After all, the majority is always right, isn't it? Not according to these boys. They had a different code of ethics by which they operated, and look at what happened:

Therefore at that time certain Chaldeans came forward and accused the Jews.

And what did they accuse the boys of doing?

"...These men, O king, have not paid due regard to you. They do not serve your gods or worship the gold image which you have set up."

Not everyone is going to agree or support your decision to do what you know is right. In fact, some will come against you because of it. But the person of integrity is not moved by the actions of others.

Then Nebuchadnezzar, in rage and fury, gave the command to bring Shadrach, Meshach, and Abed-Nego. So they brought these men before the king.

Nebuchadnezzar spoke, saying to them, "Is it true, Shadrach, Meshach, and Abed-Nego, that you do not serve my gods or worship the gold image which I have set up?"

And just look at how the three Hebrew boys reacted to the king's fury:

Shadrach, Meshach, and Abed-Nego answered and said to the king, "O Nebuchadnezzar, we have no need to answer you in this matter."

For the Hebrew boys, it was not about the king, it was about doing what they knew was right. And so they had the courage to make this public declaration:

"If that is the case, our God whom we serve is able to deliver us from the burning fiery furnace, and He will deliver us from your hand, O king."

That was bold. For all practical intents and purposes, they placed their heads in the guillotine, so to speak. They committed themselves. They had already determined what was right and now they were acting on it, even at great personal cost, by openly declaring where they stood. No one was left wondering. This alone is integrity, but they did not stop there:

"But if not, let it be known to you, O king, that we do not serve your gods, nor will we worship the gold image which you have set up."

These three boys did not base their integrity on some condition. They did not take a stand against the wrong that the king had decreed simply because they knew God would deliver them as He promises in His Word. They declared that even if God would not deliver them, they were still going to do what they knew to be right. Their integrity was such that they were willing to die for it. When one is a person of integrity, the consequences or conditions surrounding the stand one takes becomes irrelevant and immaterial.

11

Regardless of whatever else is going on, the commitment has to be honored.

> **Then Nebuchadnezzar was full of fury, and the expression on his face changed toward Shadrach, Meshach, and Abed-Nego. He spoke and commanded that they heat the furnace seven times more than it was usually heated.**
>
> **And he commanded certain mighty men of valor who were in his army to bind Shadrach, Meshach, and Abed-Nego, and cast them into the burning fiery furnace.**
>
> **these men were bound in their coats, their trousers, their turbans, and their other garments, and were cast into the midst of the burning fiery furnace.**
>
> **Therefore, because the king's command was urgent, and the furnace exceedingly hot, the flame of the fire killed those men who took up Shadrach, Meshach, and Abed-Nego.**
>
> **And these three men, Shadrach, Meshach, and Abed-Nego, fell down bound into the midst of the burning fiery furnace.**

Of course, the king was furious; so furious that he ordered the heat to be turned up. And what happened?

> **Then King Nebuchadnezzar was astonished; and he rose in haste and spoke, saying to his counselors, "Did we not cast three men bound into the midst of the fire?" They answered and said to the king, "True, O king."**

"Look!" he answered, "I see four men loose, walking in the midst of the fire; and they are not hurt, and the form of the fourth is like the Son of God."

Then Nebuchadnezzar went near the mouth of the burning fiery furnace and spoke, saying, "Shadrach, Meshach, and Abed-Nego, servants of the Most High God, come out, and come here." Then Shadrach, Meshach, and Abed-Nego came from the midst of the fire.

And the satraps, administrators, governors, and the king's counselors gathered together, and they saw these men on whose bodies the fire had no power; the hair of their head was not singed nor were their garments affected, and the smell of fire was not on them.

They were delivered and the king was amazed. This is a prime example of how integrity works.

But did you notice that their deliverance did not come until *after* they had taken a stand for what they knew was right? In fact, they were not delivered until *after* they were thrown into the fiery furnace. This is important to see because it illustrates a spiritual principle: *Deliverance does not come until after you have taken a stand.*

Look at what ultimately happened as a result of their willingness to stand for what they knew was right:

Then the king promoted Shadrach, Meshach, and Abed-Nego in the province of Babylon.

You may not have thought about it before, but these boys demonstrated integrity. They discerned what was right, they acted on it, even at great personal risk. (There certainly was a heavy price to pay.) Because they were acting based upon their conviction, they were not only delivered in such grand style, they were also promoted.

Now, let's return to the account of Daniel in the lions' den and take a closer look so that how the prophet acted with integrity is more apparent. This record is found in the sixth chapter of Daniel:

> **It pleased Darius to set over the kingdom one hundred and twenty satraps, to be over the whole kingdom;**

Satraps were rulers or leaders who acted at the behest of the king. They were like his ambassadors, emissaries or representatives.

> **and over these, three governors, of whom Daniel was one, that the satraps might give account to them, so that the king would suffer no loss.**
>
> **Then this Daniel distinguished himself above the governors and satraps, because an excellent spirit was in him; and the king gave thought to setting him over the whole realm.**

Living a life of integrity distinguishes you as being a person of excellence because you will always seek to do what is right, which ultimately is what is best. So, it is no wonder that Daniel's integrity caused him to be recognized, acknowledged, and considered for promotion.

So the governors and satraps sought to find some charge against Daniel concerning the kingdom; but they could find no charge or fault, because he was faithful; nor was there any error or fault found in him.

They were looking for something with which to charge Daniel but, because Daniel let his integrity be his guide in all his affairs and conduct, no fault could be found in him. Daniel was blameless.

Then these men said, "We shall not find any charge against this Daniel unless we find it against him concerning the law of his God."

When you have integrity, people know it. You do not have to tell anyone. Like I said, Daniel lived such a circumspect life that his enemies knew they would have to contrive something in order to accuse him of any wrongdoing – and it would have to be something in reference to his God. In other words, they could not attack him for doing anything wrong, so they had to attack him for being and doing what is right.

This is typical. When people cannot find something wrong, they will try to attack what is right. When you operate with integrity, many times your lifestyle will conflict with others. Your integrity threatens them.

So these governors and satraps thronged before the king, and said thus to him: "King Darius, live forever!

"All the governors of the kingdom, the administrators and satraps, the counselors and advisors,

have consulted together to establish a royal stat-
ute and to make a firm decree, that whoever peti-
tions any god or man for thirty days, except you,
O king, shall be cast into the den of lions.
"Now, O king, establish the decree and sign
the writing, so that it cannot be changed, according to the law of the Medes and Persians, which
does not alter."
Therefore King Darius signed the written
decree.

Again, the price tag had been attached. Doing what
was right was now going to cost Daniel something. But
look at his response:

Now when Daniel knew that the writing was
signed, he went home. And in his upper room, with
his windows open toward Jerusalem, he knelt down
on his knees three times that day, and prayed and
gave thanks before his God, as was his custom since
early days.

Daniel knew about the decree. Daniel could have
gone home, left the window closed, called upon Jehovah
in secret, and no one would have been the wiser. But he
opened his window toward Jerusalem and knelt down
three times that day — not once, not twice, but three times.
Why in the world would he do that? Because Daniel was
praying and giving thanks before his God, as was his
custom. That was what he did every day. Daniel was
consistent. His custom was not affected by the decree
that the king had signed. Right was right, and Daniel was

not going to change. The person of integrity does not change because the pressure is on.

> Then these men assembled and found Daniel praying and making supplication before his God. And they went before the king, and spoke concerning the king's decree: "Have you not signed a decree that every man who petitions any god or man within thirty days, except you, O king, shall be cast into the den of lions?" The king answered and said, "The thing is true, according to the law of the Medes and Persians, which does not alter."
>
> So they answered and said before the king, "That Daniel, who is one of the captives from Judah, does not show due regard for you, O king, or for the decree that you have signed, but makes his petition three times a day."
>
> And the king, when he heard these words, was greatly displeased with himself, and set his heart on Daniel to deliver him; and he labored till the going down of the sun to deliver him.
>
> Then these men approached the king, and said to the king, "Know, O king, that it is the law of the Medes and Persians that no decree or statute which the king establishes may be changed."

There are times when, despite how much people may want to help, and despite how powerful or influential your friends may be, you will still be on your own.

This account goes on to tell how the king lamented throughout that night for Daniel, and that he came early in the morning to check on him:

And when he came to the den, he cried out with a lamenting voice to Daniel. The king spoke, saying to Daniel, "Daniel, servant of the living God, has your God, whom you serve continually, been able to deliver you from the lions?"
Then Daniel said to the king, "O king, live forever!
"My God sent His angel and shut the lions' mouths, so that they have not hurt me, because I was found innocent before Him; and also, O king, I have done no wrong before you."

Daniel responded to the king's inquiry by telling him that God had sent an angel to shut the mouth of the lions. Why? Because he was innocent. In other words, it was Daniel's integrity that brought about his deliverance.

Then the king was exceedingly glad for him, and commanded that they should take Daniel up out of the den. So Daniel was taken up out of the den, and no injury whatever was found on him, because he believed in his God.

Just as with the three Hebrew boys, Daniel's deliverance did not come until after he stood his ground and was put into the lion's den. He first had to pay the price, but what it cost him was far less than what his enemies ended up paying:

And the king gave the command, and they brought those men who had accused Daniel, and they cast them into the den of lions; them, their children, and their wives; and the lions overpow-

ered them, and broke all their bones in pieces before they ever came to the bottom of the den.

Daniel did not need to be concerned about getting back at those who were out to get him. What Daniel's enemies had coming to them was far worse than anything he could have done of his own accord. This tells us that the person of integrity does not need to strive for vengeance against someone who has wronged him or her. Payday is coming regardless. This account in the life of Daniel ends with:

So this Daniel prospered in the reign of Darius and in the reign of Cyrus the Persian.

In looking at how Shadrach, Meshach, Abed-Nego and Daniel prospered in the face of adversity, I see an aspect of integrity that was the key to their success: Daniel and the Hebrew boys did not consider the cost. They did not consider the consequences, their circumstances, or any of the individuals involved while taking a stand for what they knew was right.

This may explain why more people are not benefiting from a life of integrity. To most, paying the price means doing whatever everyone else does. Somehow they think that doing what the majority deems right constitutes integrity. They have the "herd mentality." You can tell that they are not their own person by the way they fix their hair and dress according to what is in fashion. "Everyone's doing it;" and they have to follow suit. Jesus said in Matthew 15:14, **"...If the blind leads the blind, both will fall into a ditch."**

Whenever you allow your circumstances and the way you feel usurp your discernment, you are not able to act with integrity and will not reap the benefits. Both your decision and your integrity will be compromised. The truth must be allowed to stand above the circumstances, above any personalities involved, above friendships, and even above your own personal feelings. Your decisions must be based solely upon the intrinsic values at hand. The moment you allow your feelings or the circumstances to enter into your decision-making process, you are no longer worthy to make such a decision. The best thing you can do for yourself at this point is to step back.

It takes time to develop integrity to the point where your ability to discern between what is right and wrong is independent of the circumstances and any individuals involved. It also takes developing certain qualities or character traits that will enable you to keep your feelings from usurping your desire to discern and do what is right. Remember, *integrity* is a quality or state of being.

There are any number of character traits that will assist you in growing to the point where you can make decisions based solely on the intrinsic values at hand. But I believe the best and most comprehensive list of qualities or traits that will empower you to do what is right regardless of the situation is found in the Bible. Once you get these traits under your belt, you can make decisions based solely on the intrinsic values at hand, so that the benefits of living a life of integrity far outweigh the cost of the consequences.

THREE

THE BIBLICAL CHARACTER TRAITS

Before you can hope to stand for what is right, like the three Hebrew boys and the prophet Daniel, you must develop certain character traits. Otherwise, your ability to endure the consequences of doing what is right and reap the subsequent benefits will be severely compromised.

What follows is a listing of character traits that can be used as sort of a checklist to judge yourself. First Timothy 3:1-7 says:

> **This is a faithful saying: If a man desires the position of a bishop, he desires a good work.**
>
> **A bishop then must be blameless, the husband of one wife, temperate, sober-minded, of good behavior, hospitable, able to teach;**
>
> **not given to wine, not violent, not greedy for money, but gentle, not quarrelsome, not covetous;**
>
> **one who rules his own house well, having his children in submission with all reverence**
>
> **(for if a man does not know how to rule his own house, how will he take care of the church of God?);**

**not a novice, lest being puffed up with pride he
fall into the same condemnation as the devil.
Moreover he must have a good testimony
among those who are outside, lest he fall into reproach and the snare of the devil.**

These are the qualifications for the person seeking the
office of bishop, and the Bible goes on to name the qualities
of the deacon and even the deacon's wife. For the sake of
brevity, I have not included the traits for the deacon and his
or her spouse here. If you are beginning to see the value in
living a life of integrity, then the traits given under the head-
ing of the bishop are certainly sufficient to get you rooted
and grounded in this lifestyle.

The biblical admonition is to **remember those who rule
over you, who have spoken the word of God to you, whose
faith follow, considering the outcome of their conduct.**
Since it is a bishop (an overseer or leader), not normally a
deacon or the deacon's spouse, who rules over God's people
in terms of giving them the direction and guidance of God's
Word, I believe it is valid to recommend establishing integrity by developing the traits listed under the qualifications
for a bishop. After all, these traits dictate how the bishop is
supposed to act, and you are supposed to follow his or her
example.

The Bible lists these qualifications for bishop because
if God can get His leaders to develop these character traits,
His people will follow suit. There is a spiritual principle
involving leadership that I sum up like this: *Whatever is in
the pulpit will end up in the pews.* And the same is true with
any kind of leadership: Everything trickles down. People

naturally look to receive from their leader, and that leader can only impart what he or she already knows. After all, you cannot give what you do not have. So the leader, any leader, has to be refined before he or she is able to properly impart to others.

This means that even though these traits fall under the qualifications for leadership, you are not off the hook if you are not a leader. No one can rightfully say, "Well, I'm not in any of those positions, so this does not apply to me; I don't have to do any of this." The need to possess these traits still applies to you because even though integrity starts with the leadership, it is not supposed to end there.

I cannot find anywhere in the Scripture where God gives one standard of ethics for leaders and another for His people. And nowhere does it say that there is a special heaven and a special hell for leaders. This tells me that God expects the same out of every one of us, as far as integrity is concerned. He has no double standards.

Let me prove this. Look at the first two verses of 1 Timothy 3. What are the very first qualifications for being a bishop?

Number 1: A bishop must be blameless. Well, does this mean that a person who is not a bishop can do whatever he or she wants and not have to give account of it just because they are not in leadership? No.

Number 2: The bishop must be the husband of one wife. Well, how many wives should the usher have? How many husbands should a church hostess have?

Number 3: A bishop must be temperate. Does this mean that it is perfectly acceptable for those not in leadership to be out of control?

You may find it hard to believe that God has no double standards because society indicates that there are many different standards. But just take a look at what the Spirit of God has to say through the writings of the apostle Paul in Ephesians 4:11-16:

And He Himself [Jesus] **gave some to be apostles, some prophets, some evangelists, and some pastors and teachers,**

for the equipping of the saints for the work of ministry, for the edifying of the body of Christ,

till [or literally until] **we all come to the unity of the faith and of the knowledge of the Son of God, to a perfect man** [meaning a mature, fully developed man], **to the measure of the stature of the fullness of Christ;**

that we should no longer be children, tossed to and fro and carried about with every wind of doctrine, by the trickery of men, in the cunning craftiness of deceitful plotting,

but, speaking the truth in love, may grow up in all things into Him who is the head; Christ;

Now, this is the part of this scripture that I want you to see:

from whom the whole body, joined and knit together by what every joint supplies, according to the effective working by which every part does its share, causes growth of the body for the edifying of itself in love.

Christians are likened to joints in the human body. It says that together, all believers in Jesus Christ make up the Body of Christ, with Jesus as the head. What I want you to see is that it says, **every joint**; this means that no joint is left out. The scripture not only mentions every joint, but says that **every joint supplies**. This means that every joint — every person — has a purpose and supplies something. When some joint is not doing its part, something is not being supplied, something is not in place and therefore something is missing. If another part of the body could do that joint's — that person's — part, then that joint — that person — would not be a joint. This is why it is important that each of us be a person of integrity and not write it off as someone else's responsibility.

This scripture makes a point of letting us know that each person's life definitely affects every other life. It goes on to say that, **by which every part does its share, causes growth of the body for the edifying of itself in love.** It takes everyone doing his or her part to make us grow and realize our potential as a body of people. What one person says and does matters because none of us live in a vacuum. We all have a contribution to make, no matter who, where or what we are.

While this scripture refers expressly to Christians, the principle is the same in society as a whole. It can be tempting to believe that "I'm just one person, what difference can I possibly make." But the truth is that everyone can and does make a difference. We constantly influence and impact the lives of those around us, whether positively or negatively.

Just observe the flow of street traffic the next time you head home from work. Whenever a pedestrian ignores a crossing signal and steps into the crosswalk, the immediate oncoming traffic is forced to stop to avoid hitting that person. When these cars stop, the traffic behind them backs up. Often a car is caught in the middle of the intersection when the light changes, which impedes the flow of traffic even more.

Having said this, I think it is important to take a look at each of these traits, since people often have different ideas or definitions for the same word. All of these traits have to do with how one should conduct oneself. These traits are similar, but there are subtleties in their meanings, which shed light on what it means to truly be a person of integrity.

Trait Number One: Blameless

Some people seem to like to criticize. But as a person of integrity, people should not be able to find anything negative about your character or your lifestyle. Of course, you cannot keep people from lying about you, but your concern should be that whatever they may say is not true.

I thank God that I learned a valuable principle a long time ago. When I looked at the life of Jesus, I saw how the religious leaders of His day talked and plotted against Him. They tried to treat Him like a dog. Well, no one was more a man of integrity than Jesus. So, I had to ask myself, "How can I possibly expect to have a better track record than Jesus in terms of people not talking about me?" I can't. Once I came to the conclusion that I could not do better than Jesus, the lies that people would spread about me did not bother me.

Over the years, I have had people who do not even know me and have never met me to talk badly about me. Then, when they did meet me, they treated me like gold. To me, this is phony. But this does not mean that I have to be phony in return — and that is why I am mentioning it. I have learned to be just as sweet and nice to them as I would be to anyone else, because I know that if there is any of God's character in them, their conviction of themselves will be far worse than anything I could ever say or do. They have to live with themselves, as well as suffer the consequences of talking badly about me because there is a spiritual principle that says, **"Whatever a man sows, that he will also reap."**

Though there is no way to stop people from talking about you, the Bible does offer one sure way to help keep people from being able to lie or find fault. In the traditional King James translation of the Bible, 1 Thessalonians 5:22 says to **Abstain from all appearance of evil.** This is the best way to keep your integrity from being questioned, and it is necessary. Once there is any reason to question your integrity, you risk losing the hard-earned respect and benefits of that reputation.

Trait Number Two: Husband of One Wife

What does having one marriage partner have to do with building integrity? Commitment. Operating in integrity takes commitment, just as does marriage. If you cannot be committed and faithful to the one who shares your bed and played a part in giving life to your children, how are you going to be committed to something as intangible as integrity?

Sticking to a commitment takes giving a 100 percent — which is why most marriages these days do not last. Many married people think that their marriage is supposed to be a 50-50 proposition, each partner giving 50 percent. But it takes both spouses giving 100 percent to make a marriage work. Giving only 50 percent of yourself does not constitute making a real commitment. What you are saying when you claim to have a 50-50 marriage is that the two of you are only half committed to each other, which means that you are not really committed to each other.

Before moving on to the next characteristic, I should point out that under the New Testament, every person is supposed to have only one marriage partner at a time. The scripture says the bishop should have one wife, but the wife should only have one husband as well. This is specifically mentioned because the custom in some cultures during that time was — and still is — to practice polygamy or polyandry.

If you are doing everything you are supposed to do to take care of your mate and children, then you do not have time to be committed to anyone else. I have found in my own marriage that when I take care of my wife, she more than takes care of me. I want for nothing from her. The price I pay to be committed to seeing that she is well cared for yields awesome dividends.

28

Trait Number Three: Temperate

Temperate means vigilant. Someone who is vigilant is watchful, observant. They are constantly keeping track of things to be sure they stay on target. They never get out of control because they are always on guard, always watching.

In the Garden of Gethsemane, Jesus told His disciples, **"Watch and pray, lest you enter into temptation. The spirit indeed is willing, but the flesh is weak."** Believe it or not, He was talking about being temperate. Why? Because good intentions alone will not suffice. You need to be on guard so that you do not needlessly put yourself in situations where your bodily desires can get the best of you.

How many times have you set out to diet, for instance, only to give in to that third piece of pie?

Now, Jesus did not say that if you watch and pray you will not be tempted. You cannot live and not be tempted. What He did say was to watch and pray so that you do not *give in* to it. It is not a sin to be tempted. The Bible says in Hebrews 4:15 that Jesus **...was in all points tempted as we are, yet without sin**. So, it cannot be sinful to be tempted. But it is sinful to enter in. This is why Jesus gave His disciples — and now you — this commandment: Watch and pray. In other words, be temperate; control yourself.

Being temperate is like driving a car: You have to constantly watch the road and make adjustments, because the car is not going to stay in one lane by itself. This may seem like a chore at first, but you become accustomed to it. After you have been driving for some time, making midcourse adjustments as you drive becomes so routine that you can have a conversation with someone in the car or listen to tapes without drifting out of the lane.

You need to do the same thing with your body. If you are always watching and making the necessary corrections in your life, your body will never get so out of control that it messes up your life spiritually.

A lot of people think that Jesus was only concerned about their spiritual life. They fail to see that there is a direct correlation between what is on the inside of them and what they look like on the outside. For example, if Americans were taught to be temperate, we would not have a nation of overweight people. I know because I enjoy good food, and it seems as if everything that tastes good is fattening. But since I have been out of high school (which is more than 45 years), I have gained only four inches on my waistline. That is less than an inch every 10 years, which is pretty good. It is because I pay the price for maintaining good health by practicing temperance.

The way I keep from becoming overweight is by being vigilant — by getting on the scale every day. I have a certain ideal weight, and I do not allow myself to get any more than a few pounds over it. If need be, I will adjust my eating and exercise until my weight is back to where it should be so that it never gets beyond my control. I also watch my clothes. Whenever my clothing starts getting a little tight, I adjust my eating until they fit comfortably again. Consequently, I do not need to go on any special diets as such. I eat everything I want and still maintain a healthy weight because I use control and am vigilant about it.

First Peter 5:8 warns "**...be vigilant; because your adversary the devil walks about like a roaring lion, seek-**

30

ing whom he may devour." Now, regardless of whether or not you accept the reality of Satan, there are adverse conditions that exist in this world, which make this scripture the best news you could ever receive. Why? Because it does not say that the devil walks about seeking whom he can devour, but whom he *may* devour. In other words, you have to let him. This does not mean that the devil cannot physically devour you, but it does mean that he has to have your permission to do so. Likewise, the adverse conditions existing in this world cannot affect you unless you allow them to do so.

If Satan could devour any and every one, then he would not have to go about seeking whom he may devour. He would just do it. But he has to hunt to find someone whom he may devour. And the way he gets this authority is by our cooperation, by our not being temperate, vigilant and controlled in all areas of life.

Surely you know that overeating is harmful to your health; your body was never designed to be 20, 50, 100 pounds or more overweight. When you let your weight get out of control like that, you give the adverse conditions in the world your cooperation by providing the ammunition needed to destroy you.

Obesity causes a number of health problems. Likewise, if you smoke, the chances of your contracting lung cancer are far greater. Similarly, if you experiment with some narcotic, you heighten the chances of losing your life. This is why the Bible says to be temperate. The heavenly Father is not trying to spoil your fun; He is simply trying to protect you.

There is a price to pay for maintaining your health and part of the cost is exercising temperance. Temperance is not always easy or fun, but what you stand to gain in terms of feeling better, living longer, and being able to be more productive is well worth it.

Temperance is a trait that you either have or do not have. If you are out of control, you are out of control in some respect in every area of your life. If you are a disciplined person, you are disciplined in everything you do. You cannot be circumspect and controlled with your physical body and then be out of control with your money, or vice versa. Every area of your life eventually affects the others. I tell people that if they want to see what the inside of someone's house is like, just look inside the trunk of that person's car.

Until you develop temperance, you will always be subject to whatever circumstances surround you. Discerning what is right and what is wrong will not stand a chance in such an environment.

Trait Number Four: Sober-Minded

Sober-minded means to have a mind that is sound, sensible, controlled, disciplined and chaste; a man that has complete control over all sensual desires. This is very similar to being temperate. If your mind is not right, the rest of your life will not be right.

Throughout the New Testament, it says to be sober. So, God must be expecting us to be sober; this must be our responsibility. Otherwise, why would He mention it so often? The message He is trying to get across is that He is not going to do this for us, nor is it automatic. Being sober-minded is something we must do. This means that you and I must be the ones in control of our minds and ultimately our actions.

Take a look at 2 Timothy 1:7:

For God has not given us a spirit of fear, but of power and of love and of a sound mind.

You could put it this way:

For God has not given us a spirit of fear, but God has given us power, and God has given us love, and God has given us a sound mind.

We have the ability to be of a "sound mind" in Christ Jesus. But just because something is available to us does not make it work automatically. We still have to grab ahold of it and do something with it. Otherwise, it does us absolutely no good.

It is similar to when someone hands you a gift. They hold out a beautifully wrapped box and say, "Here, I was thinking of you. I got this for you." Unless you take that box, unwrap it, open it up and then put what is inside to use, what you have been given will never do you any good. It will just sit there, wrapped and unopened.

This is why you see so many Christians living in fear. You have to wonder why they are scared of all kinds of things, especially when they claim to know God. It seems to me that if they knew the Creator of the Universe, then there would be nothing they would be afraid of. In fact, I would think they would be rather bold.

Well, it is not that they do not necessarily know God, that they are not one of His people, that their heavenly Father does not care for and love them, or that He is not prepared to protect them, but that they are not using what He has given them. They have not unwrapped His gift. They may not even know that He gave it to them. So it can be a real challenge for them to be people of integrity, people who are consistent and who can be trusted.

When you are scared of all kinds of things, it is easy to succumb to taking the path of least resistance and going with the crowd. You think there is safety in numbers, not realizing that when you are with God you outnumber them all. When you are afraid, there are inevitably going to be times when you will see acting with integrity — doing what you know is right — as more of a case of taking a chance, than it being the guarantee that it is. And the really sad thing is, that guarantee is what you are looking for.

You have to take authority over your mind because your mind will want to run wild. Everyone's does. Controlling your thoughts takes work. This is why 1 Peter 1:13 says:

Therefore gird up the loins of your mind, be sober, and rest your hope fully upon the grace that is to be brought to you at the revelation of Jesus Christ;

The term, *gird up* means to shore up, strengthen, under gird. In other words, work with your mind. Decide that, "This is what I'm going to do, and this is what I'm not going to do. This is how far I go and beyond this point I do not go." A sober-minded person will not let his senses, emotions or desires rule him. Discerning between what is right and what is wrong stands separate from any individuals or circumstances that are involved. Therefore, the sober-minded are able to make decisions based purely upon the intrinsic values at hand. They can do this because they are in control, rather than being controlled.

Think about what this says about the sober-minded man or woman. He or she will not publicly degrade someone else, even when he or she wants to.

Of course, such a quality takes time to develop, but you will know you have arrived at being sober-minded when you do not have to really work at containing yourself.

You cannot always afford to tell people what you really think about them, especially when you have to work with them or when you have been put in leadership over them and are responsible for their guidance, care and well-being (like a parent or pastor). It is not good to lose control of your emotions, and it really takes self-control because sometimes you want to strike back. But being able to control the situation by first controlling yourself is one of the many benefits of being sober-minded.

Trait Number Five: Good Behavior

I have a very good friend in the ministry, John Cherry, who pastors a church in Temple Hills, Maryland. There is an explanation he gives when people do the horrendous things we see and hear about on the news. He says they are *misbehaving*, or they are *missing their behavior*.

Many of the young people involved in the school shootings that have shaken our nation recently come from environments where they were given no boundaries, no guidelines, no role models, and no examples to follow. They were just left on their own to go out and face the crazy world. What can you expect?

The same is true of young unwed mothers. They have no sense of value, which is why they can give away the most treasured thing they have, their body. Then, when they find out they are pregnant, they often get abortions, or worse yet, throw their babies into a dumpster.

We have a generation of young people who will do just about anything because a sense of value and ethics was never instilled in them as children. Their mothers and fathers failed to establish godly boundaries. Meanwhile, our nation is wondering how and why a kid could do such a thing, when the answer really is very simple: They did what they did because they do not have a value system to make the right value judgment. So, how could they know what good behavior is?

Good behavior starts with having the right value system. If your value system is warped, then your value judgments will be warped. If you do not have the right value system in you, you are likely to succumb to just about anything. You are *missing your behavior,* so inevitably what you do will not be right.

You can only make value judgments out of what is in you, which is why it is so important that you see yourself as the unique and valuable person that God says you are. Good behavior takes a sense of self-worth and respect that comes with seeing yourself the way God sees you. When you know you are valuable, there are certain things you just will not do.

My heart goes out to the children who have not been given the sense that they are indeed precious and valuable. No one has given them love and spent quality time with them. And so they do not value themselves. How can they then value and respect others? How can they exhibit good behavior? Spending time with children saves parents a lot of heartache and regret when they are older.

To exhibit good behavior means to be well-behaved; it means to have good conduct; to be orderly, composed, solid, honest. A person of good behavior is one whose character and conduct stand as an example or pattern for others. They are persons others can emulate and follow. That is why Paul could say to the church at Thessalonica:

For you yourselves know how you ought to follow us, for we were not disorderly among you;

Paul is saying in 2 Thessalonians 3:7, "Hey, I did not misbehave among you, so you know what is the right thing to do. I gave you an example to follow, so what are you doing *missing your behavior*?" Paul had taught the Thessalonians the Word of God. They knew what God said and thought about them — they knew they were valuable and precious. And they knew that Paul loved them because he took the effort to come and spend time with them.

Look at what else Paul wrote. Philippians 1:10:

that you may approve the things that are excellent, that you may be sincere and without offense till the day of Christ,

The apostle Paul is talking to Christians, but what he says is true for all of us. Paul says to approve things, which literally means to try or test the things that are excellent, and this is something we are supposed to do our entire lives. Paul is saying that throughout life, we constantly have to make value judgments. In other words, just being "nice" does not constitute good behavior.

Exhibiting good behavior, the type of behavior that is an example for others to follow, means making value judgments and then taking a stand for what you judge as right. This means that you have to evaluate who you are with and how they act. Are they committed to doing what is right? Is being with these people right for you? Until you are able to stand up for what you believe is right — regardless of what others think — your feelings will always affect your ability to properly discern right from wrong.

Good behavior does not mean that you are a pushover and have to put up with people who are not right. Paul told those in the church of Thessalonica to withdraw from those who were disorderly, who were *missing their behavior*.

I give the same advice to people who hang around with those who act foolishly. I tell them that they need to withdraw from those who do not want to do what is right. This means that they may have to withdraw from a best friend, a brother, sister, cousin, uncle, or even their parents. If a person knows better and yet they choose to walk disorderly, withdraw from them. This is a tough remedy.

This does not mean that you do not love people and that you are rude to them. It just means that you separate yourself from them so they are unable to influence you adversely. You still love and pray for them, you just do it from afar.

This is the price you need to pay, and it is real love, because you are setting a righteous or moral standard before them by your refusal to compromise. When you are unwilling to go down to their level, they have no choice but to come up to yours — if your fellowship means anything to them. And it is the love that you continue to extend towards them that will draw them back to you. The world needs to see examples of good behavior, and they need to see it exhibited without compromise.

Trait Number Six: Hospitable

Hospitable means to have an open heart and home, showing love or being a friend to others. To me, being hospitable means having concern, care and a loving attitude toward everyone, not just those whom you want to impress or who can do something for you. Without honing your ability to be hospitable, you will not be able to discern what is right and wrong without regard to individuals.

I believe one of the major keys to empowering you to be hospitable can be found in Romans 12:3:

> **For I say, through the grace given to me, to everyone who is among you, not to think of himself more highly than he ought to think, but to think soberly, as God has dealt to each one a measure of faith.**

Again, Paul is talking to Christians, but it applies to everyone. He says that we should not think more highly of ourselves than we ought to think. This tells us that we should think highly of ourselves, just not *too* highly.

This is important because it is the key to being hospitable. You have to think highly of yourself before you truly are able to be hospitable. It is only when you have a healthy sense of self-worth that you interface well with any and every one, because you see that no one is better than you; and, consequently, you are no better than anyone else. You have to be able to see others as your equal before you will treat them as equal. That is what hospitality is all about — treating people the way you would want to be treated.

Our society has gotten so caught up in celebrity-worship that some people have an over-inflated sense of self-worth. Their egos are fed by the way other people act around them. While I appreciate the fact that a person may have risen to a certain stature in life, the truth is that he is no more or less important than I am. We are all basically the same. If I were to stick him with a pin, he would bleed and it would hurt him just like it hurts me. So, we really are no different. The only thing that makes us different is our stature in life, which may give him more responsibility. He owes more because he has received more. Jesus said it like this in Luke 12:48: **"For to whom much is given, from him much will be required."**

Unfortunately, I run into this same celebrity mentality in the Christian church. Some people will treat my wife and me with such great respect and dignity, then go right around the corner and treat another member of our church like dirt. Every time I hear about this kind of behavior, it makes me angry because it is not right; it is phony. And here is the sad thing: I do not know which one of these actions is the real deal. Now I have to be suspect of that person. If someone treats my wife and me nicely, then treats another person in a rude and disrespectful way, something is not right. This kind of behavior certainly is not hospitable, which has to do with how you treat everyone, not just a specific person or group of people. This is how you know that a lot of people who are talking about heaven are not going there. When someone mistreats others, he is not in touch with God. He may know *of* God, but he does not *know* Him yet. For example, I know of the President of the United States, but I do not know him. I could tell you all kinds of things that I have heard about him, but I do not know the man. Likewise, people can know a lot of things about God, but not personally know Him. If they did, then they would not mistreat others. That is integrity.

The capstone is John 3:16, which says **"For God so loved the world…."** The word *world* is inclusive; it is talking about everyone, all of mankind. It is not talking about *terra firma*, or the physical planet, but about the people God created. So, everyone in God's sight is equal and the same, and He loves us all. He sent His Son to die for each of us. So, how could a person possibly mistreat someone else if he has regard for the Lord? When you truly know Him, you will have His attitude toward all people. You will not mistreat others, but be hospitable.

First Peter 4:9 says to **"Be hospitable to one another without grumbling."** This means that being hospitable has to do with more than actions, it has to do with attitude. It says to be hospitable without grumbling — without a bad attitude, not begrudgingly. The only way your attitude is going to be hospitable is if you get to the point where, like it says in Romans 12:3, you do not think more highly — or less — of yourself than you ought to think.

41

Trait Number Seven: Able to Teach

Everyone can teach, but not everyone is a teacher. *To teach* simply means to impart information. You should at least be able to share what you have learned with others. In fact, it is your responsibility to share and be able to explain what has been deposited in you by the teachers that God has set before you.

This goes along with what I was saying about the behavior of our youth. Parents are supposed to teach their children; this is part of the price of being entrusted with their care. Part of this teaching includes instilling in them a sense of value and self-worth. In other words, shipping your children off to school does not fulfill your responsibility to your children. And though you may not be a teacher as such, this does not mean you cannot impart to them values as well as information.

I have one word of caution in reference to teaching — that is, you not only teach others by the information that you give them, but also by what you do. Jesus said that you will reap what you sow. If you want people to have integrity in dealing with you, it stands to reason that you must first have integrity in dealing with them. There are going to be some people with whom you interact who you are going to have to teach integrity. And, as I said, the way you teach is by what you do, say, and how you act. A teacher is a leader.

Trait Number Eight: Not Given to Wine

When reading the Bible, you find references to drinking wine. For example, Paul wrote to Timothy instructing him to take a little wine for his stomach problem. There are also places where it talks about how both the forefathers of the faith and the early believers brought out bread and wine. But, you have to keep in mind that the people of biblical times did not drink wine as an intoxicant or as a stimulant; they drank it for the liquid. They did not have fresh bottled water or the reverse osmosis filtering system. And over long journeys in the very dry arid countryside of Palestine and throughout the Middle East, stored water would stagnate. Therefore, wine became the beverage of choice. Plus, there is a degree of medicinal value in it.

Nonetheless, look at what the apostle Paul wrote in Romans 14:21, back when wine was a vital part of man's diet:

> **it is good neither to eat meat nor drink wine nor do anything by which your brother stumbles or is offended or is made weak.**

Daniel also had something to say about wine:

> **But Daniel purposed in his heart that he would not defile himself with the portion of the king's delicacies, nor with the wine which he drank; therefore he requested of the chief of the eunuchs that he might not defile himself.**

In Daniel 1:8, the prophet called drinking defilement; Daniel refused to drink the king's wine.

This is my personal policy on drinking — and I find scriptural basis for it in what you just read — no one knows the physical makeup of an individual internally. No one knows what any individual is susceptible to. But what you do know is that there is something about any fermented beverage that has a strange effect on the physical body, the brain, and the nervous system. So, even if you do not seem to have a problem with having wine or any other alcoholic beverage, just think of the example you are setting for others — for someone who might not be able to handle it.

I take this stand because every alcoholic became an alcoholic after taking that first drink. I do not mean to imply that someone is going to turn into an alcoholic just because they had one drink. But I am saying that it is an impossibility to become an alcoholic if you never drink.

Since there are so many things you can drink to quench your thirst, no one has to drink intoxicating beverages. Therefore, I personally believe in abstaining from strong drink in any form. This is my personal belief. I will not put into my body what I know could alter my personality, my actions, as well as have a negative impact on me. When you are under the influence, you are not yourself. It is a proven fact that you do not drive or think better when you are under the influence. Only a deceived person believes such a lie.

You may say, "But I like the taste of alcohol." Well, you can develop a taste for something else to drink. In fact, you can develop a taste for anything. During the days of prohibition, people drank gasoline that was watered down with other things. The taste for alcohol is acquired. No one can tell me that when they took their first sip of alcohol, it did not taste like garbage. Despite all I have said, I do not think that being right with God hinges on whether you drink or do not drink.

What about smoking? I believe the same principle holds true. In fact, you could apply this principle to a lot of things: not given to wine, not given to smoking, not given to drugs, not given to overeating, not given to anything that can become habitual and cause you to relinquish your self-control. I say this because there is enough that can happen to harm and even destroy your body, so why heighten the odds?

For example, you may have inherited a predisposition for some disorder or disease. Drinking, smoking, using drugs, overeating — any of these destructive habits most likely will enhance this predisposition. Add to that the fact that every day, all day long, you breathe air that is polluted, especially if you are in a metropolitan area such as Los Angeles, which is where I live. And do you really know what is in your food? How about the pesticides that are used in growing fruits and vegetables? These alone wreak havoc on your body, so why deliberately put something else inside you that is poisonous? Are those few moments of pleasure really worth the damage it is doing to your body? Sooner or later, you are going to pay the price. Will that price really have been worth it?

It amazes me that people never smoke in the church sanctuary, but as soon as they get outside of the building, they light up. If it is not okay to smoke in church, why is it okay outside of the church? In all of my years as pastor, I have never seen anyone drinking a cocktail during a church service. The average person seems to have more respect for the bricks, mortar and steel girders that make up the church building than the person has for the body that God has given him.

You might be thinking, "Well, the Bible doesn't tell me not to smoke." Okay, but the Bible does not tell you to use deodorant either. Over the years, I have had so many people ask me if it is okay to smoke, but I have never had anyone ask me if it is okay to use toothpaste. Really, what these people are doing when they ask such questions is trying to find someone to agree with them so they can go on indulging in their habit with a clear conscience. They already know the answer, and they are going to be held accountable for it, regardless of what anyone else happens to say or how many people they can get to agree with them.

What it comes down to is that if something makes you someone other than who you are ordinarily, I think you ought to stay away from it or them — regardless of whether you smoke it, smell it, sniff it, eat it, syringe it. Being a person of integrity takes self-control. Whenever you are out of control, like being "given to too much wine," you inevitably compromise your integrity.

Trait Number Nine: Not Violent

The traditional King James translation uses the word *striker*, instead of "not violent." What does that mean? Not combative, not contentious or quarrelsome, not a person who strikes out and contends with others.

Please be advised: The tongue can be used to strike out at a person just as easily as you can strike someone in the mouth with your fist. I want to focus on this because your tongue can hurt someone far worse than your fist ever could. When you hit someone, that physical blow can heal relatively quickly, but the words from a verbal blow may stay with that person for years. Some people are who and what they are today because of what someone said to them 20 years ago. It can be difficult to shake the words of a striking, poisonous tongue.

I am not condoning physical abuse, but what I am saying is that words can be far more damaging. This is why I want to show you a principle found in the Word of God that can help prevent you from damaging another person for life. Philippians 2:3-4 admonishes:

Let nothing be done through selfish ambition or conceit, but in lowliness of mind let each esteem others better than himself.

Let each of you look out not only for his own interests, but also for the interests of others.

If you incorporated this into your life, then you would never spread gossip. In fact, you would not even listen to it. Nor would you ever tell something negative about someone to another person. If you really looked out for others, treating them the way you would want to be treated, then you would not be involved in any bickering, accusations, or lies. You would not have a striking tongue. As I mentioned before, you have to constantly make value judgments about things and people. But to simply talk negatively about somebody goes against the principle given in this scripture.

Not striking out against someone with your tongue, starts with the key that says, **let each esteem others better than himself.** There is no way you will treat others the way you want to be treated if you always put yourself first. It takes a conscious decision to consider others. You have to at least get to the point where you can say, "I wouldn't want anyone to talk about me, so I won't talk about anyone."

Before moving on to the next trait that ought to be in your character as a person of integrity, I want you to take a look at two proverbs. First, Proverbs 3:30:

Do not strive with a man without cause, If he has done you no harm.

This includes verbal, as well as physical confrontation. I have to ask, why would you want to strive with someone who has done nothing to you? To do this indicates there is something seriously wrong in your life.

Next, look at Proverbs 20:3:

It is honorable for a man to stop striving, since any fool can start a quarrel.

People who are in disobedience to this principle lack integrity. The implication is that they spend time talking about someone else in a negative way when they do not even know the circumstances. That is a fool! If one does not know the circumstances, how can he make a proper value judgment, which is what people of integrity are supposed to do? Besides, if a person is doing something and you are not sure that God did not tell him to do it, then you are on dangerous ground if you are condemning him. Even though you may think it is hard to hold your tongue, the repercussions you will face for not holding your tongue will be much harder to bear.

Trait Number Ten: Not Greedy for Money

In the traditional King James translation of the Bible, this character trait is described as not being greedy for filthy lucre, and so the assumption is made that money is filthy. But this cannot be true because God has mandated that His people tithe. To tithe means to give one-tenth of everything you earn to your local church or synagogue. Since people typically earn money in exchange for their hard work, then this would mean that God is requiring them to give Him something that is filthy. After all, if money is filthy, that would mean that the tithe is filthy.

Personally, I do not know anything filthy about money — except not having enough of it. People make comments such as: "So-and-So is filthy rich." I want to know why So-and-So has to be *filthy* rich — why not *cleanly* rich? For far too long, those in the church have thought there is something wrong with having money. But there is nothing intrinsically good or bad about money. It is what people do with it and how they act when they have it that is either good or bad.

Actually, this character trait encompasses a whole lot more than just money. What this scripture says in the original Greek is not to be "greedy for gain." This makes more sense, because people can be greedy for a whole lot more than just money. How about attention? Sex? Things? Friends? Position? And even recognition? All of these can be classified as *filthy lucre* when people run after them, are bad-mouthing others and running over you to get them. What this trait is referring to is being a lover of anything to gratify oneself at the expense of another.

But there is nothing wrong with gaining. You should want to gain because God says He takes pleasure in the prosperity of His servants. So how much more must He take pleasure in the gain of those who are His people? Gaining, and wanting to gain, is right. Just do not get greedy so that you look to gain at the expense of someone else or by compromising your integrity.

Keep in mind that Psalm 75:7 in essence says that promotion comes from the Lord, so you do not need to get caught up in things that will tempt you to seek dishonest gain. God will promote and prosper you. And when He promotes and prospers you, no man can take you down or take it from you (unless you let them). This means that you have got to play the game according to God's rules. You have to be a person of integrity with ethics based upon His Word. Then God will promote and prosper you — and with His blessings He adds no sorrow.

Trait Number Eleven: Gentle

Gentle means to be patient and gracious. Synonyms for gentle include: forbearance, reasonable, soft and tenderhearted.

A gentle person is one who has a tender heart — but not a stupid heart. Being gentle does not mean letting people walk on you as they would a doormat. Some people mistakenly think that to be a godly person, you have to let people spit on you, run over you, take advantage and mistreat you. That is not what my Bible says.

Yes, I know Jesus said if they slap you on one cheek, turn the other. And I also know that many so-called *macho* men have rejected the things of God because they are determined, "Ain't nobody going to hit me and get away with it." Did they ever notice that while Jesus said in Luke 6:29, **"To him who strikes you on the one cheek, offer the other also..."** He did not say what to do after that? I believe there is a reason why Jesus never said what to do next, and the reason is because after you turn the other cheek, the ball is in your court. The message Jesus is trying to get across is that you should not be so quick to strike back when someone lashes out at you. You should be gentle, reasonable and tender. You should endure what you can to pursue peace because a man of integrity is first a man of peace. This is the price you initially pay for peace.

Paul said it like this in Romans 12:18: **If it is possible, as much as depends on you, live peaceably with all men.** The very fact that Paul prefaces telling you to live peaceably with all men by saying, **if it is possible,** lets you know that some people are not going to let you live peaceably with them. Now, if you want to stand there and let someone beat you to death, that is your decision. But by saying, **if it is possible,** Paul lets you know that there is a limit to reasonableness, tenderness and being gentle. You are supposed to be gentle as long as a person allows you to be gentle. But if the person does not give you the opportunity to be gentle, then you do whatever it takes to get the job done in love — which brings me to another point.

I suspect one of the reasons why people have this false impression of what it means to be a Christian or how to conduct themselves in a godly manner is because they know that the Bible instructs people to always walk in love. I have found that most people do not understand what love really is. They think love means to always be soft-spoken with a perennial smile on your face. But who would you say is the greatest example of love in all of human history? I believe most people would admit that Jesus gave us the greatest example. But Jesus did not always walk around with a smile on His face. In my Bible, I see where Jesus was so angry that He overturned the tables of moneychangers in the temple, and it says that He even had a whip.

Did you know that in this biblical account Jesus was demonstrating love? It was love that made Jesus whip the people selling in the temple, and it was love that overturned the moneychangers' tables. Jesus was not soft-spoken about it, nor did He even ask, "Please, brethren, take these things from the temple." No. Jesus told them to get out. He called them a generation of vipers and hypocrites. This was love talking, because love always tells the truth. Jesus never bit His tongue; He always told people the truth.

It is the person who tells you the unvarnished truth who truly loves you, because it is only the truth that can set you free. If you do not know how to love this way, you will never be able to be a person of integrity, because integrity demands that you stand for what is right, despite the cost. Integrity requires love.

People also tend to mistakenly think that love means to forget how someone may have hurt you in the past because they believe that to love means to be forgiving. But forgiveness does not mean to forget what is beneficial to know. For example, say your neighbor's dog bit you the last time you stepped in their yard. To think that you should forget that their dog bites the next time you visit your neighbors (and let yourself be bitten again) is insanity.

"Well," you say, "My Bible tells me to forget about the past." Does it really? Take another look at Philippians 3:13-14:

> **Brethren, I do not count myself to have apprehended; but one thing I do, forgetting those things which are behind *and* reaching forward to those things which are ahead,**
> **I press toward the goal for the prize of the upward call of God in Christ Jesus.**

This scripture does not say **forgetting those things which are behind,** and stop there. It says, **forgetting those things which are behind and reaching forward to those things which are ahead.** The first half of what this scripture says to do is predicated upon the second half. In other words, forget those things that would hinder you from reaching forward to those things that are ahead. That is what you are supposed to forget — not what can be beneficial knowledge and experience for making progress.

You are supposed to forget the fact that you were abused and mistreated as a child, that your best friend let you down or, worse yet, betrayed your trust. You are even supposed to forget the fact that you had an abortion or were responsible for someone having an abortion. Yes, it should never have happened, but your remembering it will not change it.

This is the determining factor of whether or not you should forget something in your past: Dwelling on it is not going to change the fact that it happened, and if you keep dwelling on it, you will never make progress. You are supposed to forget all the past that would hinder you from reaching forward to those things which are ahead.

Forgetting those things which are behind could not mean to forget the past entirely. Otherwise, Jesus is the biggest violator of this scripture because He said to eat the bread and drink the cup to show His death until He returns. He tells you to do it in remembrance of Him. If what Paul was saying means that you are supposed to forget everything in your past, then why not forget the fact that Jesus was crucified?

And if you are supposed to forget the past, why does God tell us in the Bible what David did thousands of years ago? Because He uses it as an object lesson for His people — and you should do the same with your past. This understanding of love and forgiveness should help you to see that committing to the Lord does not mean that you no longer stand up for yourself and just let people take advantage of you.

To be gentle means to be patient and gracious. This does not mean simply sitting around, being cool while waiting for what you want. It entails doing whatever you can, to the very best of your ability, while waiting — even despite of the circumstances. Yes, having the ability to wait a long time is part of it. But, from a scriptural point of view, patience means endurance or the ability to endure.

Patience is what perfects the ability to execute integrity. Jesus said it like this in Luke 21:19: **"By your patience possess your souls."** Your soul is what makes you the unique person you are. Your soul is comprised of your will, your emotions and your intellect. What Jesus is saying here is that you control who you are as a person by exercising patience.

And notice, Jesus says *you* possess your soul by your patience — not that God will possess your soul. This tells you that developing patience is your own responsibility. So, patience is not something you pray to receive from God. It is something that must be developed. It has already been given to you — like having a sound mind — but it is not automatic. The only way to develop it is by being patient.

Not a whole lot of people have developed patience. Far too many let their soul run them. That is why they are in all kinds of trouble. They have financial problems, sexual problems, interpersonal problems, and even self-esteem problems, because they have not learned to possess their souls. They are not in control of themselves, so how can they execute good value judgments and integrity? It is only through patience that you learn the kind of self-control needed to possess your soul (control your will, emotions and intellect) so that you can live a life of integrity.

This same correlation between patience and possessing your soul is expressed in James 1:1-4:

> **James, a bondservant of God and of the Lord Jesus Christ, To the twelve tribes which are scattered abroad: Greetings.**
>
> **My brethren, count it all joy when you fall into various trials,**
>
> **knowing that the testing of your faith produces patience.**
>
> **But let patience have its perfect work, that you may be perfect and complete, lacking nothing.**

Various trials refers to the temptations, trials and tests that everyone faces. Temptations, tests and trials are a fact of life. The scripture does not say to count it all joy *if* you fall into various trials, but *when* you fall into various trials.

These various trials serve a specific purpose: God allows these various trials so that as you trust and do what His Word says to overcome these various trials, they develop you. You have to learn somehow, and this is how. After all, how do you know what you can take? You don't. You do not know what you can stand until you actually stand and see the results of having stood. This is character development that happens only over time.

So, as this Scripture goes on to say, **let patience have its perfect work.** This should read "perfecting work," meaning *maturing,* because that is what is happening as you endure — you are maturing. Do not thwart this process and flake out so that you short-circuit your growth. The saddest thing in the world is to see someone 50 or 60- years-old acting like a 3-year-old. Without this aspect of your character together, you will not be able to handle the challenges that come without blowing up and subsequently destroying all that you have worked so hard to obtain. You will never be effective in helping others or in anything you do.

Hebrews 10:35-36 also shows how important patience is:

> **Therefore do not cast away your confidence, which has great reward.**
>
> **For you have need of endurance, so that after you have done the will of God, you may receive the promise:**

The original King James says that you have need of patience. Patience and endurance are synonymous in this case. Endurance is the ability to stand, and then having done all, to stand. Why? So that you receive the promise — the benefits — that comes from doing what you know is right. Patience is part of the price to be paid in terms of being a person of integrity.

Let's see how patience ties right in with being gracious and forbearance that enables you to be a gentle person. Romans 12:9-12 says:

> **Let love be without hypocrisy. Abhor what is evil. Cling to what is good.**
>
> **Be kindly affectionate to one another with brotherly love, in honor giving preference to one another;**
>
> **not lagging in diligence, fervent in spirit, serving the Lord;**
>
> **rejoicing in hope, patient in tribulation, continuing steadfastly in prayer;**

To be gracious means to be marked by kindness and courtesy, and we see this expressed in the first three verses of this scripture. A gracious person is one whose love is genuine and whose concern never fails to be for the best interests of others. This kind of person is, as well, **patient in tribulation**. In other words, he is able to endure adversity. He is not the type to get up and leave when the going gets tough.

Being **patient in tribulation** means enduring whatever comes against you, but it does not mean to just stand there and allow someone to destroy you. It means having a long fuse instead of a short one, and that your hope is always that the other person will back off. However, if the person keeps pushing, then I believe there is a time to stand up for yourself.

God is this same way. He only lets things go for so long and so far, then He moves in judgment. He let the wickedness of the people in Noah's day go for a long time before the flood came and destroyed them all. God had a very long fuse, but He did not let the people's mess go on forever. Likewise, Judgment Day is coming. It may not seem like it is because God is long-suffering, patient and able to put up with a lot — the same way He expects us to be. But this does not mean He will allow what is wrong to continue forever — and neither does He expect you to put up with being wronged, with being mistreated and abused, indefinitely.

Trait Number Twelve: Not Quarrelsome

The King James Bible translates *not quarrelsome* to *not a brawler*. What Paul was telling Timothy is that the bishop or leader, and consequently the people, should not be contentious or given to fighting in the sense of being the aggressor. Part of the ideal and standard that Paul was holding up before Timothy is that the man or woman of integrity is a person of peace and always under control — one who maintains composure and will not go off in anger. This kind of person is deeply touched by any unrest, controversy or disturbance and, consequently, will work to bring peace and unity.

It is only fitting that as a person of integrity, you strive to have peace rather than striving against others and causing confusion. You ought to be at peace with others as well as with yourself because the heavenly Father is a God of Peace. Just look at what Paul wrote in 1 Corinthians 14:33:

For God is not the author of confusion but of peace, as in all the churches of the saints.

It could not be any plainer than this; God is the author of peace.

Having said this, I want to point out that in this scripture there are two extremes given: confusion and peace. Neither one of these extremes just happens. James 3:16 says that **where envy and self-seeking exist, confusion and every evil thing are there.** In the King James translation, it says that envy and strife are what bring confusion and every evil work. In either case, confusion is the result of something. A person has to do something for there to be confusion and, likewise, a person has to do something for there to be peace.

This explains why 1 Peter 3:10-11 says:

For "He who would love life and see good days, Let him refrain his tongue from evil, And his lips from speaking deceit.
Let him turn away from evil and do good; Let him seek peace and pursue it."

We are told to seek and pursue peace. In other words, peace has to be sought; it does not just happen.

So, you do not sacrifice integrity or morality and ethics to have peace, as some would suggest. You are not supposed to simply let the status quo be the status quo, when the status quo is wrong — that is not how to have peace. Many mistakenly think that it is, but they are, like I said, mistaken. Going along with whatever someone else wants is not doing what the scripture says and pursuing peace – it is just letting things go.

In fact, this is a dangerous thing to do. There are people who will take advantage and run right over you. They need to be stopped. Every person should not have his way, and so your job is to resist him. Sometimes you have to resist hostility in order to arrive at peace. This is how you seek and pursue peace.

Challenges will not go away by themselves. There are ungodly things going on now that never would have gotten to this point if people of integrity had acted responsibly and gotten involved instead of just standing by — hoping and a praying — while letting things go. Now there is a mess. Integrity demands that you stand for what is right despite the cost. Of course, you do it in love and with as long a fuse as possible.

People say, "Why talk about such and such a problem, we'll never get rid of it." With that kind of attitude, they are absolutely right. We will never get rid of the evil and injustices in our society if we never confront them. We will never get rid of them if we allow them to run their course. Integrity confronts wrongdoing.

God does not expect us to put up with everything to have peace. When Paul told Timothy that part of the standard was not to be quarrelsome, he was not saying to never fight. After all, he admonished Timothy to **fight the good fight of faith**. Since Paul was writing under the unction of the Spirit of the Lord, God must not be opposed to fighting; it just depends upon what kind of fight and who is involved. And even though Jesus is the Prince of Peace, nowhere in the Bible does it mention anyone pushing Him around. Jesus had a long fuse. But once He moved, He moved decisively. We need to be the same way.

We need to realize that whatever we allow in our lives, God has no choice but to allow because He has given us a free will. Besides, this earth is our home — not His. If something needs fixing in our lives or in this world, we are the ones who will have to fix it. It will never get fixed if we have the kind of attitude that assumes things cannot be made better. Just because we do not already see a certain thing being done, does not mean that it is impossible to do.

And forget about trying to pray away every adversity. If it did not get there through prayer, it is not going to leave just through prayer. I am not saying that prayer will not help, but that sometimes things have to be confronted. We have to confront the wrong that we see. Sometimes we will have to fight a war to get peace.

Some people, who do not know very much about the things of God, will think I am advocating violence and trying to stir up trouble. Their whole concept of godliness is to be a doormat, letting others do and say what they want.

But in reading and studying the Bible, you can see that it was never in God's plan and purpose for anyone to enjoy anything but peace. In fact, 2 Corinthians 13:11 tells us that the very nature of God is love and peace. Yet it is up to us to do what it takes to have peace in our lives, our families, our communities, and in the world. Whatever we tolerate is what we will have. The heavenly Father has done His part; He has given us a standard and instructions as to how to achieve that ideal in the Bible. And part of that standard is to be at peace.

Throughout the Bible, we are admonished to be people of peace. Ephesians 4:1-3 says:

> **I, therefore, the prisoner of the Lord, beseech you to walk worthy of the calling with which you were called,**
>
> **with all lowliness and gentleness, with longsuffering, bearing with one another in love,**
>
> **endeavoring to keep the unity of the Spirit in the bond of peace.**

And Psalm 34:14 says, **Depart from evil and do good; seek peace and pursue it**, which is very similar to what we read in 1 Peter 3:10-11.

The reason both the Old and the New Testaments tell us to pursue peace is that it is a universal principle. There are spiritual principles that were peculiar to the Old Covenant; they began and ended there. There are some that are unique to the New Covenant; they begin and stay there. Then there are others that have universal application, which can be found throughout the Bible. They have and will always be in operation. Peace is one of them.

So you see, having peace — not being quarrelsome — is what God has in mind for us. But just because we are not supposed to be the aggressor, does not mean that we are supposed to be passive. We are to endeavor to be in the bond of peace. The ball is in our court.

Trait Number Thirteen: Not Covetous

When most people hear the word *covet*, they typically think of the commandment that says, "Thou shall not covet thy neighbor's wife." But covetousness is more than just wanting what your neighbor has; it is the constant pursuit of things at the expense of what is truly important. It is an insatiable desire for worldly gain, a desire that is never satisfied and that leaves you unhappy and unfulfilled.

Many times, covetousness manifests itself in greed, specifically in a person who becomes a lover of money. But it is not limited to money and possessions. People can become covetous of attention, recognition, someone else's position or status, or another person's talent and abilities. If left unchecked, covetousness can become all-consuming and lead you to forgo integrity.

Covetousness is different from greedy for gain in that it is dangerously deceiving. It causes you to think "Boy, once I get that, then I'll be happy and satisfied." But the problem is, that "thing" is never enough. By the time you get it, something new or better is on the market. Or, that thing you thought you wanted turns out to be more trouble than it is worth.

I know because this has happened to me. I used to think I wanted certain things, like the very latest electronic gadgets, and I would not be happy until I got them. Then, once I got them, I wished I did not have them.

You cannot afford to allow the acquisition of things to get ahold on you, because then you will be spending your life getting things. You will get to the place where you no longer have things, but those things will have you. You see people like this all the time. They make hundreds of thousands of dollars and are as much in debt as they were when they made only a hundred dollars, because the pursuit of things has them.

People ask me how they can know the difference between having a godly desire for something better in life and being covetous? After all, there is nothing wrong with wanting the best in life. Well, the answer is simple: Are you jumping through hoops to get it? Is what you think you want keeping you up at night or preventing you from enjoying what you already have? Is the pursuit of that object consuming all your time and energy?

These are all signs of covetousness, but the way to really tell is by what you are doing with what you already have. Are you overspending, living on credit, living beyond your means and thereby forfeiting your future for the present? Some people say, "Boy, if I had a million dollars..." and they run to stand in line to play the lottery. They are out of control, so they are hoping to hit it big and get themselves out of the hole they have dug for themselves. They see that million dollars as their answer. But if they were to win that million, they more than likely would end up just as broke — if not worse — because all that money would do is afford them the opportunity to be even more out of control and irresponsible.

I can say this with certainty because covetousness is a negative character trait. Remember what Jesus told His disciples? He said that those who are faithful in little will be faithful in much. Covetousness works the same way. People do not stop being covetous just because they have obtained what they wanted. It will not be long before they want something else, something more. It is a never-ending cycle.

So how do you overcome covetousness? First John 2:15 tells us, **Do not love the world or the things in the world....** *World*, in this case refers to the world system, meaning the system that operates within our economy. If you are not careful, this system will not only trap you, but will keep you entrapped.

How? By appealing to your senses, your desires and emotions. This system operates by constantly making people dissatisfied and unhappy with what they have. The wheels of industry are always inventing new things and designing new styles that can make a person feel as though they are missing something if they do not buy one. Advertisers are constantly sending messages that suggest, "You're losing out — everyone's got one, everyone's doing it."

The way to avoid falling into the trap of running out to buy something you do not need or really want is to recognize that the thought, "I've got to have one of those," is just in your mind. It is not necessarily true. You do not have to have one. In fact, chances are, that thing will only leave you dissatisfied, unhappy and unfulfilled.

In other words, be sober-minded. Refuse to think about having what everyone else has. Take control over your mind, over your thought life, by not giving these ideas — often implanted in your conscious by advertisers — validity and life by dwelling on them. Otherwise, you will overspend. Then your ability to operate with integrity will be compromised because you are dependent upon the world's economy and can no longer afford to stand up for what you know is right since you cannot risk missing a day's work.

This is why the scripture says not to love the world. Whatever a person loves, they will give themselves to. Whatever someone loves, he will end up making commitments to. The scripture says not to love the world because its economic system is not going to love you back. It is not designed to give you comfort. In fact, it is set up to keep you hung up and strung out. So do not commit to the world by becoming indebted to it.

Now, this scripture does not say not to use the world. In other words, there is nothing wrong with wanting to benefit from what the world has to offer, just as long as you do not fall into its trap. This is why Jesus told His disciples in Luke 12:15 to **"Take heed and beware of covetousness, for one's life does not consist in the abundance of the things he possesses."** He is saying to be vigilant, temperate – exercise self-control. Using what the world has to offer to benefit you without becoming indebted and trapped takes being sober-minded. It takes recognizing that things are not going to make you happy, because there is more to life than just material possessions.

The business world has made it very easy to become indebted to the economic system. "No payments until next year" is the biggest trap ever set for those who are not sober-minded and temperate. I know this firsthand because I have been there. It looks like six months from now everything will be fine and there will be the money to pay the thing off. So you sign the paper, get the product, and then it seems as if six months or a year later comes tomorrow and there is still no money to pay for the thing. Now you are scrambling to find a second job in order to make the payments. You wanted your future now and it is killing you.

The way to work the system — to use it to your advantage — is to wait until you physically have the money for whatever product you may need or desire that is being offered with the no payments for six months or a year. Then go ahead and sign the purchase agreement and receive delivery. In the meantime, bank that money so it is collecting interest until the time comes to pay. This is so simple that it seems obvious, but just look at how many people are over their heads in debt.

I use credit cards in much the same way. I take advantage of the convenience and safety of not having to carry a lot of cash. The monthly statements I receive also help me to keep better track of my spending over the course of a month. But I never purchase things with my credit card that I do not already have sufficient funds to cover. This way, at the end of every month I am able to pay off my existing balance without accruing any finance charges.

I believe covetousness is mentioned so many times throughout the Bible because it affects more than just you; it affects your family. Your actions bind them up unfairly. There was a time when I had to have the very latest in electronics. I loved gadgets and I put my family in debt by using credit cards to purchase them. Then it came time to buy shoes for our little girls and I complained for days. I could not believe their feet had outgrown the shoes I had bought them two years prior. When my wife informed me that the children also needed new clothes, I almost hit the ceiling. Those electronics had such a hold on me that having the very latest was more important to me than providing for my wife and children.

When others are dependent upon you, sheer common sense dictates that you should not buy or do things without weighing all the factors is involved. You have to stop to consider: "If I do this, then will I be able to do that which I've already committed myself to doing?" Unfortunately, people lose their rationale when they get into covetousness. They become so consumed with getting things that all they think about is, "Wow, I have to get this right now; I'll make ends meet somehow." They never consider how it is going to impact their future or others around them, such as their families. And by future, I am not talking about 20 years from now. The future oftentimes is just two weeks or a month away.

The seventh chapter of the Old Testament Book of Joshua gives a perfect example of how covetousness led to a bad judgment call that affected an entire family. This situation occurred just after the children of Israel entered the Promised Land. God had delivered the great city of Jericho into their hands and they were instructed to utterly destroy the city, neither taking nor leaving anything except that which was stipulated for the temple treasury.

But not everyone heeded the voice of the Lord. Look at what Joshua 7:2-5 says happened the next time they went into battle:

> **So about three thousand men went up there from the people, but they fled before the men of Ai.**
>
> **And the men of Ai struck down about thirty-six men, for they chased them from before the gate as far as Shebarim, and struck them down on the descent; therefore the hearts of the people melted and became like water.**

Ai was a small city. The men of Israel should have had no trouble taking it. When Joshua sought the Lord as to why they suffered such a humiliating defeat after such a grand victory, he learned that someone had disregarded the orders pertaining to the destruction of Jericho. One man's actions caused the death of 36 men and the defeat of an army. Joshua was eventually led to the man who had disobeyed. This is what that man, Achan, had to say for himself:

"**When I saw among the spoils a beautiful Babylonian garment, two hundred shekels of silver, and a wedge of gold weighing fifty shekels, I coveted them and took them. And there they are, hidden in the earth in the midst of my tent, with the silver under it.**"

Why did Achan take of the spoils? Covetousness. Look at the end result of his coveting:

Then Joshua, and all Israel with him, took Achan the son of Zerah, the silver, the garment, the wedge of gold, his sons, his daughters, his oxen, his donkeys, his sheep, his tent, and all that he had, and they brought them to the Valley of Achor.

And Joshua said, "Why have you troubled us? The LORD will trouble you this day." So all Israel stoned him with stones; and they burned them with fire after they had stoned them with stones.

You may be thinking, "But that doesn't seem right. That was unfair and unjust of God to make Achan's family pay for what he did." Well, there is a price to pay for disobedience. Besides, if things had been different and Achan had inherited land and lots of money, his family would have partaken of that inheritance. It works both ways.

Coveting results in poor judgment that adversely affects not only you, but your family, your spouse, as well as your children and loved ones. This is why it is dangerous and why you need to watch what you do. Many of the things in society today are the result of yesterday.

For example, I have heard young men say, "I am never going to get married. I don't want a family; I don't want the responsibility." They go out partying and, in the process, abuse and misuse the body God has given them. They sleep with any and every one they find attractive and willing. Five or ten years pass and here comes Miss Right. Now their heart is throbbing. They want to get married and enjoy a normal married life, but they have dissipated their body. They cannot produce children. Or, they have contracted some sexually transmitted disease. So, what you do is important not only to you, but to your posterity.

The Bible also tells of what happened to Saul, the first King of Israel, when he lacked the integrity to do what he knew was right. First Samuel 15 tells of Saul being instructed by the prophet Samuel to attack the city of Amalek and destroy all that was in it. So Saul went ahead and took this city, but he spared Agag, its king, and all that was good. Later, when confronted by Samuel, Saul tried to pass the blame on to the people, saying they took what should have been destroyed. But he was the king; he was the one responsible.

When this did not work, Saul went on to claim that his sin was that he feared the people and obeyed their voice, instead of doing what he knew was right. In other words, he simply let the majority rule; he did not let his own discernment stand separate from the individuals involved. God held him accountable.

While integrity can promote someone to a position of leadership, a lack of integrity will result in their downfall as a leader. Samuel told King Saul that because he did not do what was right, he was no longer fit to be king. It was only a matter of time before David replaced Saul as king, and Saul's entire family, except for Mephibosheth, was destroyed. Undoubtedly, Saul would have been a lot better off if he had not succumbed to covetousness. Surely these goods were not worth forfeiting his kingship.

See how deceptive covetousness is? It can seduce you into forfeiting everything you have worked so hard to gain just for that one thing or one moment of pleasure that you think will make you happy, change your life or fill the void that only God can fill. You can even be the king and have it all, yet covetousness can still destroy you. Regardless of your position in life, covetousness works the same way. This is why I say that 1 Timothy is not meant exclusively for the church leadership.

The epitome of covetousness is found in the account of Judas selling Jesus to the Pharisees for 30 pieces of silver. Judas was motivated by greed. And what happened? His end was not good; Judas' covetousness drove him to suicide.

Ananias and Sapphira, according to the fifth chapter of the Book of Acts, did not fair any better:

But a certain man named Ananias, with Sapphira his wife, sold a possession.

And he kept back part of the proceeds, his wife also being aware of it, and brought a certain part and laid it at the apostles' feet.

But Peter said, "Ananias, why has Satan filled your heart to lie to the Holy Spirit and keep back part of the price of the land for yourself?

Wait a minute! Ananias went to the apostles and laid at their feet part of the money he had received for the sale of his property. But Peter asked why he lied to the Holy Spirit. This does not make sense — except that when you lie to God's leaders or to His people, God sees it as lying to Him. And, while you may be thinking that you are getting away with something, you cannot lie without eventually having to give an account of it.

Peter goes on to point out in Acts 5:4-5:

"While it remained, was it not your own? And after it was sold, was it not in your own control? Why have you conceived this thing in your heart? You have not lied to men but to God."

Then Ananias, hearing these words, fell down and breathed his last. So great fear came upon all those who heard these things.

And the young men arose and wrapped him up, carried him out, and buried him.

I do not know how Ananias died, but I do know that the man dropped dead on the spot. Look at what happened to his wife, Sapphira, in Acts 5:7-11:

Now it was about three hours later when his wife came in, not knowing what had happened.

And Peter answered her, "Tell me whether
you sold the land for so much?" She said, "Yes,
for so much."

Then Peter said to her, "How is it that you
have agreed together to test the Spirit of the
Lord? Look, the feet of those who have buried
your husband are at the door, and they will carry
you out."

Then immediately she fell down at his feet
and breathed her last. And the young men came
in and found her dead, and carrying her out,
buried her by her husband.

So great fear came upon all the church and
upon all who heard these things.

Why do you think they died like that? What was their
sin? They had acted as if they had brought all they had received from the sale of their property.

Certain people in the church at that time were selling
the surplus they had and putting all the proceeds into a common pot. Ananias and Sapphira sold what they had as well.
But they kept back part of the money from the sale, yet
acted as if they were giving all of it. They lied.

Peter pointed out that it was theirs in the first place,
so they did not have to lie. All they had to do was say
"Look, we got so much for this and we are putting in
only half. We're banking the other half. We're with you
halfway." But they acted as if they were giving 100% of
what they had profited from the sale of their property.
Why would they do such a thing? Because they wanted
to keep part of the money they had made and still be en-

titled to the same share as the others who had given 100% of what they had profited. They tried to deceive, out of greed and covetousness. And they ended up with half of the money and died. That is not worth it.

Covetousness eventually leads to destruction of some sort. It may not come as quickly as it did for Judas or Ananias and Sapphira. It may not be revealed publicly, as in the case of Achan and King Saul, but Judgment Day is coming. It may result in the destruction of a friendship, or the loss of financial security, a job, your self-respect, your reputation, or your family's admiration. But payday is coming, and the price you will pay is not worth it.

To avoid this kind of destruction, you must recognize that life is not all about things and that you do not need everything you see. Secondly, at some point, you must exercise self-control. Otherwise, when you get to the point where you are making the amount of money you desire, you will squander it because covetousness will drive you to buy everything you see. You will end up just as broke as you were when you did not have much money.

As my good friend John Cherry also says, "You have to get to your godly point of satisfaction." This does not mean you do not have desires or cannot like nice things. It does not mean that you do not want to someday acquire a better and more luxurious car, or a larger house with a better view. But getting these things should not leave you so strung out that you do not enjoy life, your family, friends and the things that you do have because you are so tied up in adding to your collection of things.

Getting to your godly point of satisfaction means that you are satisfied with having everything you need and desire, so that you are not wasting your resources obtaining more of what you do not really need and really want.

Trait Number Fourteen:
One Who Rules His Own House Well

People get the idea that to rule means to be a dictator sitting on a throne giving out commands. Or, they have this image of someone with a big whip, ordering people about. *Rule* literally means to stand in front of and lead. When the Bible says to rule your own house, it means to walk in front of your family in such a way that their natural response is to follow you. This has to do with how you carry yourself. You do not — and should not — ever have to pull out a whip and declare that you are the head of your home.

I never had to tell my children that I am the head of my home. I never have had to tell my wife, either. I just live in such a way that they know I *am* the head. I walk like it, I talk like it, and most importantly, I act like it. I make provisions as if I am the head of the house. Therefore, I do not have to say it because I am it. Unfortunately, most people who are saying it are not it, and that is why they have to say it. But those who are truly the heads of their homes do not need to tell anyone.

Integrity begins at home. If a person does not conduct himself with integrity in relating to his spouse and family, he is not going to have integrity in the affairs of others. This is why, when I want to know what a man is really like, I look at his wife and children. Is his wife happy? Are she and their children being provided for? Are they in control or are they out running the streets? Your family learns from the example you set. And the way a person is at home is usually the way he or she truly is, because it is when you are at home, in the privacy of your own sanctuary, that you "let down your hair," so to speak. That is when the real you comes out.

My wife and children will tell you that I am the same at home as I am at work or standing in the pulpit. This kind of "transparency" lets people know they are dealing with a person of integrity. You have to be suspicious of someone who acts one way with their family, another with friends, and yet another with business associates. Which is the real person? Integrity leaves no room for doubt or wondering. When you are dealing with a person of integrity, you know right where he stands and who he is.

Trait Number Fifteen: Not Puffed Up With Pride

Pride is a conceited sense of superiority, of thinking you are better than everyone else. I have already mentioned that you cannot be hospitable if you are caught up in pride. Pride is the root of racial and ethnic prejudice, and the Bible has much to say about it.

Proverbs 11:2 says:

When pride comes, then comes shame; but with the humble is wisdom.

And Proverbs 16:18 warns:

Pride goes before destruction, and a haughty spirit before a fall.

This certainly is what happened to Lucifer. Whether you believe he is real or not, he is the classic example of pride run amok. Isaiah 14:12-15 has this to say about him:

"How you are fallen from heaven, O Lucifer, son of the morning! How you are cut down to the ground, You who weakened the nations!

"For you have said in your heart: 'I will ascend into heaven, I will exalt my throne above the stars of God; I will also sit on the mount of the congregation on the farthest sides of the north;

"I will ascend above the heights of the clouds, I will be like the Most High.'
"Yet you shall be brought down to Sheol, to the lowest depths of the Pit.

Satan is Lucifer. God created Him. He was the most beautiful angel, and was called the anointed cherub that covers until he became prideful and challenged God by saying that he was going to **"be like the Most High and ascend above the heights of the clouds."** This was the epitome of pride. Lucifer lost his anointing (the power of God) because of it.

Take a look at the vision of the prophet Obadiah, recorded in the first chapter of the Old Testament book bearing his name:

The vision of Obadiah. Thus says the Lord GOD concerning Edom (We have heard a report

from the LORD, And a messenger has been sent among the nations, saying, "Arise, and let us rise up against her for battle"):

"Behold, I will make you small among the nations; You shall be greatly despised.

The pride of your heart has deceived you, You who dwell in the clefts of the rock, Whose habitation is high; You who say in your heart, 'Who will bring me down to the ground?'

Though you ascend as high as the eagle, And though you set your nest among the stars, From there I will bring you down," says the LORD.

The principle enumerated in these passages is the same that is found in Isaiah: Pride leads to self-exaltation, and you do not want to exalt yourself, nor do you need to. The Bible promises that God will exalt you in due season. Let God do it and no man will be able to demote you. But if you promote yourself, as Lucifer tried to do, chances are you will end up demoted.

I think people who try to push themselves have low self-esteem and a sense of insecurity. They do not think very much of themselves, so they believe they have to keep themselves in front of people.

When you feel right about yourself from the standpoint of the Word of God, you do not feel a need to promote yourself because your sense of self-worth is not wrapped up in some position or in what man thinks. Your true self-worth comes from God alone, in knowing that He loves and values you enough to have given you His very best, His Son Jesus.

Now, despite how bad a picture the Bible paints of pride, there is another extreme that is equally as detrimental. While some people have an inflated sense of superiority, others have an inferiority complex. They have no sense of self-worth and so they suffer from low self-esteem. I know. I struggled with low self-esteem for years because I was brought up in an environment that told me that I was nothing, I could achieve nothing, and therefore would not succeed at anything. I was written off, never even given a chance. I know I am not alone in this. There are far too many people who have been beaten down by life and society, sometimes by their own loved ones. In some family circles, the saying goes "Your granddaddy was a rat, your father was a rat, and you're going to be a rat just like them."

Consequently, children who grow up hearing these kinds of remarks, having this attitude expressed towards them, have a hard time dealing with other people because they have no sense of self-worth and self-respect. A person cannot possibly have respect or see others as valuable when they have no respect for themselves and do not think they have any value. It is no wonder that children in the ghetto — and now even in the suburbs — are shooting each other.

It does not matter what ethnic group a person is, or in what geographical area they live. I have had the privilege of traveling all over the world and I can tell you that people are the same. They may speak a different language, have a different accent or look different, but they are all basically the same. Everyone needs to be loved, appreciated, and thought well of, regardless of who they are. I think God built this into our system when He created us, and therefore we need these things to give us a sense of well-being.

79

That is why every person needs to evaluate himself according to what the Spirit of God had Paul write in Romans 12:3:

For I say, through the grace given to me, to everyone who is among you, not to think of himself more highly than he ought to think, but to think soberly, as God has dealt to each one a measure of faith.

We looked at this scripture before, but it bears a second look because a lot of people miss the truth of what this passage is saying.

Highly is generally used to distinguish from *lowly*, so it seems reasonable that we should think highly of ourselves, just not *more highly*. Not more highly in respect to thinking we are better than someone else, but that we have respect and care for the unique individual that God created us to be. After all, God certainly thinks highly of each of us. He thought enough of us to send His only Son to redeem us. He could have sent an angel, but He sent Jesus. So having low self-esteem cannot be right in the eyes of God. He thinks highly of us, and we must think highly of ourselves.

The question then arises: Out of what crucible do you generate thoughts about yourself? From where should these *high* thoughts come from? I submit that they should come from your covenant with God.

This is where the Word of God comes in. You need to find out what God thinks of you by learning and then believing what He says about you in His Word. You should think highly of yourself, not because you are and have all of this in manifestation, but because of what God says.

I found out who I am in Christ by studying the Book of Romans through the Book of Jude in the New Testament. These books of the Bible are His messages to His Church, while the four Gospels are the historical account of the earthly life of Jesus and the Book of Acts is the history of the establishment of the Church. Of course, the Book of Revelation deals with eschatology, meaning the end of all things. You have to expressly study the epistles of Romans through Jude to discover for yourself what God says about you. Then, out of this knowledge, you should develop your character, from which your integrity should flow.

As you do this, you will begin to see yourself the way God sees you and it will elevate your expectancy level. Take, for instance, favor. When I go places, I expect to be treated with favor because I am royalty. First Peter 2:9 says:

> **But you are a chosen generation, a royal priesthood, a holy nation, His own special people, that you may proclaim the praises of Him who called you out of darkness into His marvelous light;**

As a believer, the Bible says I am part of a royal priesthood. Therefore, I am royalty. Later, upon reading and studying the rest of the New Testament, I found the reality that I am royalty confirmed in Revelation 19:14-16, which says:

> **And the armies in heaven, clothed in fine linen, white and clean, followed Him on white horses.**
>
> **Now out of His mouth goes a sharp sword, that with it He should strike the nations. And He Himself will rule them with a rod of iron. He Himself**

treads the winepress of the fierceness and wrath of Almighty God.

And He has on His robe and on His thigh a name written: KING OF KINGS AND LORD OF LORDS.

Jesus is the King of kings and the Lord of lords; kings and lords are both plural. Before making the connection between 1 Peter 2:9 and what this scripture says, I had always thought this was referring to earthly kings. I pictured a man sitting on a throne, wearing a big beautiful ermine robe and a crown, with people waiting on Him hand and foot. I had no idea that the kings the Bible is talking about are those who have accepted Jesus Christ as their personal Savior and Lord.

The Bible confirms this again in Revelation 1:5-6. And, in talking about Jesus, Revelation 5:9-10 says:

And they sang a new song, saying: "You are worthy to take the scroll, and to open its seals; for You were slain, and have redeemed us to God by Your blood out of every tribe and tongue and people and nation,

And have made us kings and priests to our God; and we shall reign on the earth."

So you see, I have been elevated to the position of a king and priest. And this has helped me to keep my life straight.

If you view yourself as trash, then you will act that way. You will think, "What difference does it make? I'm trash anyway." You will make yourself available to anyone and anything that comes along.

Once I realized that I am royalty, there were certain things I would no longer do because a king would never do such a thing. Likewise, there are a lot of things that you will have an entirely different view about once you begin to see yourself the way God sees you. There will be certain things you will not do because you know that you are better than that. And this makes your ability to live a life of integrity and be an example for others to follow a whole lot easier.

Of course, this is dependent upon whether you take the Bible personally. It has made all the difference in my life. It changed my attitude and expectations. And I found out that a lot of things that happened to me were the result of what I expected, because that was where my faith (my ability to act on the Word of God) was. And so I got what I expected.

Ever since my expectations have risen to the level of what God says about me, I have seen that what He says about me having favor is true. I have favor, and I never have to ask for it. I do not have to go out of my way to get it; it comes to me like filings drawn to a magnet. But it has to do with who I have on the inside — Jesus Christ.

I must forewarn you that those who do not have knowledge of what the Bible actually says about God's people will be offended by you. They will think you are the biggest egotist in the world because you walk with confidence. The problem is not with you, but with them. They have seen so little confidence in their lives that they do not know it when they see it. They assume it has to be arrogance because they are looking at you through eyes colored by low self-esteem. They simply do not know who and what God made them to be. But I refuse to let their ignorance hold me back from believing and acting on what the Word of God says.

Unfortunately, most people take their cue from what other people say or think about them. They always try to please people, when life would be so much easier if they concerned themselves with pleasing God. I know because I used to be like that. Now I know that pleasing God is a whole lot easier than trying to please people. Life has gotten so good for me that I simply cannot afford to let what others think keep me from doing and being all that God has said.

When you know what God has to say about you and see yourself that way, you will not have the kind of pride that makes you think you are better than someone else. If you do get into pride, it is only because you have left God's standard and started to develop your own. You need to think highly of yourself, just not more highly than you ought.

Trait Number Sixteen: A Good Testimony

The best way to explain what it means to have a good testimony is to say that having a good testimony involves having a reputation of integrity.

If someone were to talk to the people with whom you work, what would your co-workers have to say about you? They do not have to be Christians, nor do they have to like you. But they should not be able to say anything negative about your character or lifestyle. They should not be able to find a legitimate fault. They should not be able to say, "Well, you know that person's word is not worth a dime. They will lie in a minute." This is a bad report.

I found out over the years that people watch you and that your actions are what they notice more than what you say. They notice the little things. They may not say anything about it at the time. Five long years could pass and you end up working with them and they still remember. Then, one day you get up enough nerve or find the right situation where you can reach out to them in friendly companionship. And what happens? They bring up what they saw you do five years ago.

If you do not have a good testimony among people, your integrity will be suspect and people are not going to trust you. Nor will they open up to you. They will not be inclined to stand by you in times of challenges — or just plain support you. They are not going to readily accept your leadership. That is why I say that leaders lead by example, while their integrity sets that example.

Having a good testimony equates to having a reputation for integrity. Earning this kind of a reputation takes possessing and exercising with wisdom all the traits I have just shared and explained. Perhaps this is why having a good testimony is the last of the character traits that Paul mentions to Timothy.

The Second Witness

Before moving on, let's take a quick look at Titus 1:7-9. This passage of scripture also lists the ideal characteristics or standard for being a bishop. I think this is important, since there is a biblical principle that Jesus expressed when He said: "... **'by the mouth of two or three witnesses every word may be established.'"** What this means in terms of the Bible is that any truth you see in one part of the scripture, you will find expounded upon in at least one other passage. And it is this consistency that authenticates any revelation you think you see in God's Word.

> For a bishop must be blameless, as a steward of God, not self-willed, not quick-tempered, not given to wine, not violent, not greedy for money, but hospitable, a lover of what is good, sober-minded, just, holy, self-controlled, holding fast the faithful word as he has been taught, that he may be able, by sound doctrine, both to exhort and convict those who contradict.

Many of the traits or attributes listed here are the same or very similar to what we just examined in 1 Timothy. Both 1 Timothy and Titus begin by stating that a bishop must be blameless. They both go on to specifically mention being sober-minded, hospitable, not being given to wine, not violent, and not greedy for money.

The only real difference between 1 Timothy and Titus that I can see is that while 1 Timothy starts by primarily emphasizing the character traits you should have as a leader and person of integrity, Titus focuses first on how you should not conduct yourself. But all the characteristics these two passages list are basically the same, and when combined together, they paint a portrait of the person of integrity. So there can be little doubt that this scripture is a witness to the importance of possessing certain character traits.

I have taken the time to examine these traits with you because many profess to be people of integrity, but you would never know it judging from their character. What they say does not go with how they act. Jesus said that every tree is known by its fruit. An apple tree will always produce apples; you will never find a lemon growing on an apple tree. So if you say you are a person of integrity, then one ought to be able to see the fruit of this in the way you act. These traits are like a mirror. A mirror allows you to see yourself; you do not usually use a mirror to see someone else. And this is precisely what an understanding of integrity in light of these character traits does for you. These traits enable you to judge and see for yourself what you look like — who you really are.

What fruit are you growing? For example, if you say that you believe in Jesus, then why would you not act like it? Jesus said that if you love Him you would obey His commandments. This is why I say that integrity is a mirror – because through integrity you can see if what you profess to have and know is for real.

Integrity demands that you examine yourself. It is what causes you to question things and to seek the truth – even when it comes to yourself. I believe the Apostle Paul was alluding to integrity when he told the church at Corinth in 1 Corinthians 11:31, that **"...If we would judge ourselves, we would not be judged."** I believe he says this because once you judge yourself, your integrity should cause you to act on what you know is right so that you become blameless. Jesus said it like this in Matthew 7:1, **"Judge not, that you be not judged."** He expounded on this in verses 3 through 5:

> **"And why do you look at the speck in your brother's eye, but do not consider the plank in your own eye?**

Or how can you say to your brother, 'Let me remove the speck from your eye'; and look, a plank is in your own eye?

Hypocrite! First remove the plank from your own eye, and then you will see clearly to remove the speck from your brother's eye."

So you see, integrity is a personal thing. It starts with you. Before you can execute the principles of integrity effectively so that you come out ahead in the midst of adversities that challenge your integrity, you have to have developed these traits out of which comes integrity.

FOUR

SETTING YOUR STANDARD

Now that you know what integrity is, you need to know how to implement it in your life. Go back to 2 Thessalonians 3, where the apostle Paul is admonishing the saints at Thessalonica. In Verse 7, he has this to say about his own behavior as well as those who traveled with him:

For you yourselves know how you ought to follow us, for we were not disorderly among you;

Paul basically says, "Hey, I did not misbehave among you. I demonstrated good behavior; I did what was right." The only way Paul could say this about himself and those who traveled with him was that he obviously had made a decision to do what was right long before he ever arrived in Thessalonica. He must have made a conscious effort to do right; otherwise, how could he have known with any certainty that his behavior was above reproach? Whenever you make a blanket statement like that, there are people who will take it as a challenge to find fault.

I can relate to what Paul is saying because I determined a long time ago that there were certain things I was not going to do. I made up my mind that if any member of the congregation I pastor makes a mistake, he will never legitimately be able to point his finger at me and say, "Well, if Fred had not lived such a shoddy life, I would have done better." No one was going to be able to say that about me because I had made a commitment to live right. This is not to say that I am better than anyone else, or that I am perfect. Nor that I innately have some God-given capacity to do what is right. But I have found out that living a life of integrity boils down to making a decision. What I do or do not do is simply a matter of choice.

The Lord God Himself, the Creator and Sustainer of the Universe, says in Jeremiah 31:34, when talking about Israel, **"...I will forgive their iniquity, and their sin I will remember no more."** Have you ever wondered how God, the One Who Knows All, can cease to remember something? Is the Bible actually saying that God just forgets about sin? I have to ask this question because, if so, then what else might He be forgetting? Well, the answer is that God does not forget; He just *wills* not to remember. He *wills* it. It is as simple as that — just a matter of will.

And the same holds true for you. God has given mankind the precious gift of free will. We exercise this privilege the same way God does, by the choices we make, by what we will to do. It is a matter of our will. No other physical entity on this planet has the ability to determine its lifestyle and destiny by what they will to do. This is an awesome gift, as well as an awesome responsibility. We will one day have to give account for it. So you want to be sure to exercise your will wisely.

So how do you *will* to live a life of integrity? What decisions do you have to make? What do you have to choose to do?

You Must Set Rules

You have to govern your life in such a way that you cannot act without integrity, even when you might want to. You do this by setting rules for yourself and following them without exception.

These rules have to be based on a standard you ascribe to in life that does not change, regardless of the circumstances or consequences. Your standard has to be something higher than the circumstances, because circumstances come all the time.

These rules have to be made known to the appropriate parties involved. As I already mentioned, one of the three components of acting with integrity is to let people know where you stand. Likewise, you have to let your loved ones and the people you work with know where you stand in terms of the standard and rules you have set for yourself since they are likely to be the ones helping you to follow or carry out these rules. They will also hold you accountable, which will help you to stay on track.

And these rules have to be set before circumstances arise so that you are prepared to deal with them. If you wait until you are in the midst of a challenge to decide how you are going to handle it, you are likely to come up with all sorts of ways to compromise.

Also, never leave room for second-guessing or thinking twice about the rules you have made. Stick to them. Be true to the standard you have set for yourself.

For example, part of my standard is not to be greedy for gain. I base this on the character traits listed in 1 Timothy, which is part of my standard. The rule I have set to be sure I stick to the standard of integrity that I see given in the Bible is that I always play by the rules. Even if no one else does, I will. It does not matter; I refuse to gain dishonestly by circumventing the rules, because to me this is being greedy for gain.

Now, as a minister, I am considered self-employed by the federal government of the United States. So I am responsible for paying my own taxes, just like the person who owns his own business. Throughout the year, I get a lot of money handed directly to me because people appreciate the gift that God has placed in me and how that gift has affected their lives in a positive way. Of course, it is not me; it is the Lord that they appreciate. But since they cannot physically give anything to Jesus and say, "Lord, thank You," they give it to His servant or those who represent Him.

I am at the point now where this is almost a constant thing. People will walk up, shake hands with me, and leave a hundred dollars in my hand. Of course, I do not know what it is at that moment. I just shake hands, realize they have given me a piece of paper (it could be a note or it could be money), and I put it in my pocket. I never look at it right there. I say, "Thank you," and go about my business until I am home.

No one knows what the person has given me except that person, me, God and the devil. The IRS does not know. Usually there is no record because it is a cash transaction. So, there is no paper trail, no canceled check. Over the course of a year, this can add up to a lot of money. I could choose not to report this money, so that I would not have to pay taxes on it. This would save me a considerable amount since I am in a tax bracket where I have to give the government 53 percent of my earnings.

But I have a little book that I keep, like a mini-pocket planner, in which I write down every single dollar I receive. I make a record of it. I am not required to do this as such. Yet, I do. So there is now a record, and this enables me to keep close track of how much money I receive so that I can be sure to pay the appropriate taxes on it. This may seem a little extreme, but I do not go to bed at night wondering if or when the Internal Revenue Service is going to come knocking on my door.

Another similar illustration has to do with being on television. Let me preface this by saying that the U.S. Postal Service knows who I am. When writing to me, people do not have to write a street address on their envelope. Just as long as it says Fred Price, Los Angeles, California, it will end up at the church because the post office is so accustomed to getting mail from all over the world for me and the ministry. In the mail comes money for the support of the television program. Most of the checks that come in are made out to Fred Price. Very few people make their donation payable to Ever Increasing Faith Ministries, which is the name of this television ministry.

This means I have to make a judgment call, because sometimes people send money and their desire is for me to have it personally. They will write a note that says something like, "This is for Drs. Fred and Betty to go to dinner."

So I made up a rule years ago. Unless otherwise indicated, whenever any money comes into the church as a result of the television ministry of Ever Increasing Faith, it automatically goes to cover our television expenses. I do not care if it is $12 million. No questions asked; it goes to pay television expenses.

I do not even think about it. Why? Because if I did, I could come up with all sorts of reasons why the money must be for me. So I do not even open the door for that temptation to come in. Setting this, and other rules like it, has enabled me to keep the ministry's financial matters right before God. I do not have to be concerned about one day being accused in the high court of heaven of stealing God's money. And because this foundation has been laid in my life, it is that much easier for me to exercise the discipline needed to keep the rest of my finances in order and under control.

Another rule that I have made to not be greedy for gain is that I will not imitate the success of others. Of course if the Lord tells me to do it, then I make an exception to this rule. Otherwise, I am not going to do something because it looks as if it is causing someone else to prosper. I am going to do what I am called by God to do. I am going to do what is reasonable.

A lot of times people see that something is working for someone else and decide to do the same thing. They neglect their own dreams, desires and plans to pursue what someone else has. I am not saying that is it wrong to glean from the success of others, nor am I suggesting that you have to reinvent the wheel. But what I am saying is that you should not just jump on the bandwagon. It is important to fulfill your God-given purpose — not someone else's. The world does not need any carbon copies.

Part of integrity is sticking to your game plan, to your purpose, or to what God has placed in your heart, and how you plan to accomplish that purpose. You have to be careful not let someone else's success lure you off track. Your ultimate success and fulfillment in life will come from doing what you are meant to do. This is why I do not waste time looking and comparing myself to any other ministers. I am an original — and so are you!

Can you see how setting rules and making it a point to be a person of integrity has enabled me to remain in a highly visible ministry position for more than 25 years without one scandal? Do you see how setting a standard along with rules has helped me to stay on track in terms of what God has called me to do? If I can do this in ministry, you can set similar rules in your own life and profession. The principle I have just shared can be applied in your home, to your family, your children, your spouse, your business, your job, and your associations. Regardless, the principle works the same — whether on a large or small scale.

Setting rules for myself and taking care to follow them has benefited me greatly. For one thing, I have developed a habit of doing what is right; so acting with integrity has become automatic — like driving a car. I do not have to think anymore about what is the right thing to do in certain situations because I usually just do it. I never find myself wondering what to do given the circumstances, and this has made living a lifestyle of integrity much easier.

Another benefit is that I have developed such a keen sense of my conscience that I cannot play any roles. This has helped me in two ways.

Number 1: I am always myself, so I know I could not do anything out of my character without someone noticing.

Number 2: I cannot put on an act because I really do not know how to be any other way than what I am. So, I really have no choice but to do what I know to be right because I would be no good at hiding any wrongdoing. Both of these points are things you consider when you are tempted to do what you know is wrong.

Unfortunately, many people are so used to putting up a front to cover themselves that they have gotten good at it. It is almost the natural thing to do because it has become such a habit. They have to really concentrate on doing what they know is right whenever they feel that it is important.

But for me, the opposite is true. It is easier to tell the truth. I say this because when you lie, you have to remember what you said and then everything else in your life has to line up with that lie in order to have any hope of keeping others from discovering the truth. It takes a lot of energy and effort to do this, especially when you are not used to it. That is why it is easier for me to admit that I made the mistake, do whatever I need to correct it, and go on with being free to be myself.

Because I have set and followed rules for such a long time, I also benefit from having a sensitive conscience. This is good in that I know I would end up telling on myself if I did something wrong because I would have no peace. No minute of pleasure or any dishonest gain is worth giving up the ability to sleep at night. And this alone protects me from giving in to a lot of temptations.

Consequently, there is no way I could go to bed at night next to my wife after I had been intimate with another woman. I just could not — not because I am incapable of it, but because my conscience would not allow it. This kind of sensitivity has kept me from ruining my marriage, and this has been the ultimate payoff for me for living a lifestyle of integrity.

My children and most of my parishioners can and will tell you that my wife is probably one of the sweetest, most loving and beautiful women you could ever hope to meet. She has been nothing but a blessing to me. But my flesh is just like everyone else's. I have had opportunities — opportunities that my flesh wanted to take. So, I thank God that He gave me enough sense to know that I needed to set some rules for myself.

The only reason I have shared these personal examples with you is so that you can see that no one is immune to temptation. I am just like you. If you want to be a person of integrity, you have to use wisdom and protect yourself by — among other things — setting a standard and corresponding rules for yourself. If you will take the time to do this, those rules will go with you the rest of your life. If you govern yourself by them and let them direct you, they will simplify your life and keep you out of all kinds of trouble by helping you to avoid unnecessary temptations.

What I am recommending *can* be done. Setting rules *does* work, and choosing to be a person of integrity *does* pay off. If I can do it, then you can too. I am no better than anyone else. Like me, it is just a matter of your will, of your choice, of deciding to do it.

Acting as if You Are Dead

The next step in implementing a lifestyle of integrity is to "act as if you are dead." This is scriptural, and it is the key to the solution of any problem. Whether it is a physical problem with your body or a mental problem, Colossians 3:5 is your solution. God has made it so simple:

> **Therefore put to death your members which are on the earth: fornication, uncleanness, passion, evil desire, and covetousness, which is idolatry.**

God tells you to put to death your members. What are your members? Members are parts of your body, your appendages — things that are attached to your body. For example, your finger is a member, your arm is a member, and your foot is a member.

Obviously God is not telling you to kill your body in the literal sense, because that would contradict what is found elsewhere in the Bible. So the key to understanding what this scripture is saying must lie in what it goes on to enumerate:

> **fornication, uncleanness, passion, evil desire, and covetousness, which is idolatry.**

Wait a minute! Fornication is not a member. But it takes a member of your body to commit fornication. So what this scripture must be telling you to do is to put that desire to fornicate to death by considering that member which it takes to commit it as if it were already dead.

I am sure this sounds strange at first, but just think about it for a moment. If your sex organs were physically dead, you would not have a problem with fornication, would you? In fact, I do not think the opposite sex would want you. If you were to visit your local cemetery, you would not find dead people committing fornication. So, it stands to reason that if you were to act as if your sexual organs were dead, you would not have a problem with fornication.

Since God tells you to put such things as fornication to death, this is your only option. The only way you are going to be able to put fornication to death is by acting as if you are dead, because you see yourself every day and know that particular appendage is very much alive. Nonetheless, you act as if it were dead. It does not matter how you feel. You do it because God's Word tells you to do it, not because you feel like it. And once you do, you will not have a problem with fornication.

What about covetousness? This scripture mentions it, so how do you put that to death? Well, what leads you to covet something? Your eyes. Covetousness starts with what you see.

Remember the examples of covetousness found in the Bible? Achan confessed to Joshua that he saw the accursed things, and what happened? He coveted and took them. If Achan had been blind, he would have never seen those things and would not have coveted and taken them. And how was King Saul able to claim that the people took only the good of the spoil that they were supposed to destroy? Because of what he saw.

The same thing is happening today. A lot of people are in trouble financially because of all the buying they have done of things they saw. And what is worse, they continue to add to their debt. As soon as they see something, they start thinking about it. Then their adrenaline starts flowing, their juices begin generating, and they are as good as sold — trapped by what they saw!

Blind men usually do not have any problems with covetousness. And neither would you, if you were blind. It would not matter how many new models the manufacturers came out with, you would not even know the difference because you would not see them to know.

So what do you do? You put that member, your eyes, to death by acting as if you are blind. You have to act as if you do not see things that you know you would want if you stopped to look at them. If you will do this, you will stay out of trouble. Otherwise, things will have you. First, thoughts about the thing will come, then the passion, and it is only a matter of time before you will take action and are trapped.

You have to realize that your body will always crave things, and that the wheels of industry know exactly what buttons to push to get this response out of you. If you are not in control, you will go with the flow, taking the path of least resistance, and end up in debt and financially strapped – at the very least.

You see this with credit cards. Most people who have credit cards do not realize that their credit cards actually have them. They are living beyond their means and cannot afford to miss one day's salary without jeopardizing their ability to pay some bill. I know because I used to be the king of overdrawn credit cards. And after I got out of credit card debt, I got rid of my credit cards and would only pay cash for things. But that was not the solution either, because I was still out of control. You are in control only when you can have a credit card and use it without it using you. However, wisdom dictates that if you have to get rid of that card until you get some control, then get rid of it.

Just because your body is craving something does not mean you have to give it what it wants. Your body does not need everything it craves. In fact, everything your body wants is not always good for it. You may be craving that last piece of pie, but you have already had nine other pieces.

"Pastor, it just feels right" someone might say. Well, just because you feel like doing something does not make it right. Feelings do not validate actions. Just because I may feel like punching your lights out does not make my doing that right. Just because sex feels good, does not make fornication right, either. Contrary to popular opinion, you do not have to do everything you feel.

Dead people do not have cravings. Dead people do not have feelings. As a matter of fact, dead people do not get their feelings hurt. So if you act as if you are dead, you will never end up offended with someone and make a bad situation worse by acting ugly.

The way to overcome the personal challenges you may be facing is to consider yourself as dead. You need to recognize that whatever has you climbing the walls is able to do so by appealing to at least one of your senses — what you see, hear, taste, smell, touch or feel. So if you were to act as if you were dead, then your senses could not be used against you. Act as if you are dead — this is the way the person of integrity fortifies himself against sin.

You Must Be Willing to Stand

How often do you hear those engaged to be married make comments such as, "I really love my fiancee, more than life itself. So and so is my dream; all that my heart has longed for." They cannot wait to say "I do," and then it seems that before you know it they cannot wait to say "I don't."

The reason there are so many divorces today is because people typically say "I do" until the challenges come. They do not want to stand and pay the price. They do not want to be inconvenienced, which tells me that they were never really committed. Standing takes commitment — the kind of commitment that comes from having a deep conviction.

It is easy to spout off and say you are committed to something when there is no pressure. But the true test is when the challenges start. This is when reality is revealed. You can never know whether you are acting from a deep and steadfast principle until that principle is challenged, and if you are never challenged, you never really know how deeply you believe it. Not really.

People will only stand and fight for what they truly believe in and are committed to. The three Hebrew boys said that even if their God did not deliver them, they would not bow down to the golden idol that the king had made. Daniel went to the lions' den rather than cease praying and worshipping his God. If something is important enough to you, then you will do whatever it takes to see your way through the circumstances. You will pay the consequences. Incidentally, this is when you find out whether you really ascribe to the standard you have set for yourself. This is where the rubber meets the road. I point this out because where there is no possibility of its loss, integrity cannot exist. Integrity is something that is proven.

For instance, I have heard people say, "I believe in telling the whole truth and nothing but the truth." But when their bank mistakenly credits them with an extra $100, they take advantage of this mistake. They rationalize what they know to be wrong by telling themselves "What's $100 to the bank? They have more money than I do." People with this kind of an attitude are only fooling themselves. This is not integrity; they are not standing for what is right. In fact, without realizing it, they have just put a price tag on something that is supposed to be priceless — their integrity!

Integrity causes you to stand when everyone else is seated. It is not a game of musical chairs. If you are a person of integrity, you will be willing to bear the challenges to your convictions even when it is difficult and the consequences are unpleasant. You will not change your stand because of the circumstances. Like Daniel and the three Hebrew boys, what is happening around you is irrelevant and immaterial, since it is beneath your dignity not to stand for what you believe.

Everything in life has a price tag. You are going to pay one way or another. Either you pay in terms of the consequences that you endure when taking a stand for what is right, or you pay in terms of forfeiting the benefits that come from doing what is right.

FIVE

WHAT'S IN IT FOR YOU?

Integrity is valuable and will work to your benefit, as long as you develop it through positive character traits and implement it in your life. But there is one more factor that I would like to present for your consideration. And this factor, I believe, is the most important of all. Actually, I have mentioned it throughout this book since it is the key to your ultimate success. It is your life insurance policy. Your guarantee.

What is this factor? God and His Word. When you factor God into the integrity equation, you not only will pay less and come out ahead, but you have a guarantee to come out on top of your situation. You have God's Word on this. Hebrews 11:6 promises:

But without faith it is impossible to please Him, for he who comes to God must believe that He is, and that He is a rewarder of those who diligently seek Him.

God is a rewarder of those who not only believe that He is, but who also believe that He is a rewarder of those who diligently seek Him. God is a rewarder! And His blessings add no sorrow. I know this is true because He has rewarded me and the ministry I pastor.

For example, the Lord had given me an assignment to teach on racism in the church. This is not a popular subject and many of my colleagues and friends in the ministry turned their backs on me and even spoke against the message I had been given. People who I thought were my friends left me, and I was out there on my own to say what God had given me. I was accused by some as being everything but a child of God.

But at the same time, people who I did not know rose up to defend and support me. I received two highly regarded national awards and the ministry began to prosper like never before. New doors to teach were opened to me. It has been an awesome experience and I thank God for allowing me to have a part in helping to right a hideous wrong. But all of this would never have happened if I had not taken a stand for what I knew was right and done what God had assigned me to do.

Throughout the New Testament, I see what Paul endured for the sake of telling the truth of Jesus Christ. Paul wrote in 2 Corinthians 11:24-28:

> **From the Jews five times I received forty stripes minus one.**
>
> **Three times I was beaten with rods; once I was stoned; three times I was shipwrecked; a night and a day I have been in the deep;**
>
> **in journeys often, in perils of waters, in perils of robbers, in perils of my own countrymen, in perils of the Gentiles, in perils in the city, in**

**perils in the wilderness, in perils in the sea, in
perils among false brethren;**

**in weariness and toil, in sleeplessness often, in
hunger and thirst, in fastings often, in cold and
nakedness;**

**besides the other things, what comes upon me
daily: my deep concern for all the churches.**

Despite all of these trials and persecution, what was Paul's
concern? He was concerned about the churches that God had
called him to establish. He was concerned about fulfilling his
course in life. Consequently, he did not allow any of these
hardships to stop him from fulfilling his purpose in life.

I also see that Paul sang while imprisoned, shook the
poisonous snake from his hand, and even rose up after he
had been stoned. Paul always triumphed in the end. In fact,
in 2 Timothy 4:6-7, the King James translation records Paul
writing to his son in the ministry:

**For I am now ready to be offered, and the time
of my departure is at hand.**

**I have fought a good fight, I have finished my
course, I have kept the faith:**

Although history records Paul as having been beheaded
by the Roman government, Paul says he had completed his
mission in life. He succeeded in life. In fact, he prefaced this
by writing, **"I am now ready to be offered."** So, Paul chose
to die.

This is supported by Acts 21:13, when Paul spoke to
those who had come to warn him about the danger of his
going to Jerusalem:

Then Paul answered, "What do you mean by weeping and breaking my heart? For I am ready not only to be bound, but also to die at Jerusalem for the name of the Lord Jesus."

Paul completed his purpose in life and he determined how he was going to die. That is pretty awesome when you think about it. Often people get so caught up in the way this apostle died that they overlook that it was his decision. They see it as a failure rather than the triumph that Paul said it was.

And just think about this: Paul wrote two-thirds of the New Testament. Next to Jesus, he has probably influenced more people's lives than anyone else since his time all because he remained on course and lived for what he knew was right. Paul was dedicated to God.

Joseph was another man that the Bible records as having integrity that was grounded in a desire to please God. Joseph was the favorite son of Jacob, and his brothers, out of jealousy, sold him into slavery when he was a teenager. But take a look at how he acted in the face of adversity, as recorded in Genesis 39:

Now Joseph had been taken down to Egypt. And Potiphar, an officer of Pharaoh, captain of the guard, an Egyptian, bought him from the Ishmaelites who had taken him down there.

The LORD was with Joseph, and he was a successful man; and he was in the house of his master the Egyptian.

And his master saw that the LORD was with him and that the LORD made all he did to prosper in his hand.

So Joseph found favor in his sight, and served him. Then he made him overseer of his house, and all that he had he put under his authority.

So it was, from the time that he had made him overseer of his house and all that he had, that the LORD **blessed the Egyptian's house for Joseph's sake; and the blessing of the** LORD **was on all that he had in the house and in the field.**

Thus he left all that he had in Joseph's hand, and he did not know what he had except for the bread which he ate. Now Joseph was handsome in form and appearance.

And it came to pass after these things that his master's wife cast longing eyes on Joseph, and she said, "Lie with me."

I want to stop here to ask a question: What were the chances that Potiphar's wife would have told her husband she was having an affair with Joseph? Chances are, she would have said nothing because she would have been very happy with what she was getting. After all, Joseph was handsome in form and appearance. Joseph would then have had everything his Egyptian master had.

This says a lot about the person of integrity. Joseph had an open invitation to take advantage of the situation, but remaining faithful and trustworthy was obviously more important to him. Likewise, a person of integrity does not take advantage of a situation or avoid the cost of doing what he knows is right. His integrity is independent of the circumstances; it is about being trustworthy, not about what can be gained or lost.

But he [Joseph] refused and said to his master's wife, "Look, my master does not know what is with me in the house,
and he has committed all that he has to my hand.
"There is no one greater in this house than I, nor has he kept back anything from me but you, because you are his wife. How then can I do this great wickedness, and sin against God?"

Wait a minute! This woman was not God's wife; she was Potiphar's wife. But Joseph did not answer, "How can I do this great wickedness and sin against my master who has entrusted me with everything in this house?" No, He said, **"How then can I do this great wickedness, and sin against God?"**

You would think that Joseph's refusal would have been out of fear or loyalty to his Egyptian master. After all, Potiphar had given him great authority and commanded a position of power and respect within the land. But Joseph's allegiance was to God, the real source of his position in Potiphar's house. Integrity is a natural byproduct of one's commitment to God.

So it was, as she spoke to Joseph day by day, that he did not heed her, to lie with her or to be with her.

Potiphar's wife was after Joseph day after day, but he remained consistent and steadfast in his commitment to doing what was right in the eyes of God. The scripture says that Joseph went so far as to not be around her. Integrity leaves no room for evil to take root; it fortifies against temptation.

But it happened about this time, when Joseph went into the house to do his work, and none of the men of the house was inside,

Joseph's master was not there; in fact, no one was there. So, who would know? God would. Joseph would — and he would have to live the rest of his life knowing the wrong he had done. Integrity does not do what is right just because someone is watching.

that she caught him by his garment, saying, "Lie with me." But he left his garment in her hand, and fled and ran outside.

And so it was, when she saw that he had left his garment in her hand and fled outside,

that she called to the men of her house and spoke to them, saying, "See, he has brought in to us a Hebrew to mock us. He came in to me to lie with me, and I cried out with a loud voice.

"And it happened, when he heard that I lifted my voice and cried out, that he left his garment with me, and fled and went outside."

So she kept his garment with her until his master came home.

Then she spoke to him with words like these, saying, "The Hebrew servant whom you brought to us came in to me to mock me;

"so it happened, as I lifted my voice and cried out, that he left his garment with me and fled outside."

So it was, when his master heard the words which his wife spoke to him, saying, "Your servant did to me after this manner," that his anger was aroused.

111

> **Then Joseph's master took him and put him into the prison, a place where the king's prisoners were confined. And he was there in the prison.**

Joseph's integrity meant more to him than anything else; so he acted on it, and it cost him something — his freedom. Joseph was thrown in jail. His master's wife trumped up charges, telling her husband that Joseph tried to rape her, all because Joseph would not give her what she wanted. And his master just took his wife's word for it, regardless of Joseph's track record. Integrity will cost you something, but it pays off in the long run because although things looked really bad for Joseph...

> **...the LORD was with Joseph and showed him mercy, and He gave him favor in the sight of the keeper of the prison.**

Because he acted with integrity and maintained his commitment to God, the Lord honored Joseph by making the best for him in the worst of situations:

> **And the keeper of the prison committed to Joseph's hand all the prisoners who were in the prison; whatever they did there, it was his doing.**
> **The keeper of the prison did not look into anything that was under Joseph's authority, because the LORD was with him; and whatever he did, the LORD made it prosper.**

And the Lord did not stop there. If you are familiar with the life of Joseph, you know that God used this situation to position Joseph to become the second greatest man in the entire Egyptian empire and to save his family in the time of great famine.

God raised Joseph up because Joseph did what was right in the eyes of the Lord, even at great personal cost. Joseph remained faithful all the way down the line. And so, God saw to it that it paid off for him. Just look at what Joseph had to say when all was said and done. In Genesis 50:18, his brothers came to make amends, and verses 19 and 20 record:

> **Joseph said to them, "Do not be afraid, for am I in the place of God?**
>
> **"But as for you, you meant evil against me, but God meant it for good, in order to bring it about as it is this day, to save many people alive."**

You could say what Joseph tells his brothers this way: "Look; I'm not going to judge you. Even though you meant to harm me, God has turned it all around for good. We all are much better off."

Joseph's response is important because he verbalized a spiritual principle that, in essence, promises that what the devil means for harm, God is able to turn around for good. God can and will turn your adversities into triumphs. What an awesome promise to be able to claim.

But you can only stake this claim and reap its many benefits when, like Joseph, your integrity is based on an allegiance to God and to doing things His way. Whenever you act with integrity out of a desire to please God, you will end up further ahead. You may look to be down for a few counts, but you will ultimately come out on top. This is why acting with integrity, especially out of regard for God, is so important.

Keeps You Out of Trouble

I had a similar experience. When my wife, Betty, was going through cancer, there was a lady who used to come to every church service. She made sure that I noticed her and even got so bold as to sit in my wife's usual seat. She would stick around after service and always walked out when I was leaving. She made it a point to pass right in front of me, so I could observe her from behind. She would even park her car directly behind mine.

That was what I call an opportunity. I share this with you to give you a real-life, modern-day example of how opportunities present themselves to you. I knew what this lady was offering — a "freebie" — although it would have been the most expensive thing I ever paid for.

You will always be tempted, tried and tested – that is a part of life. There will always be opportunities. It is not that there are opportunities that matters, but what you do with them. Opportunities come. If you say that you are never tempted, then you are the biggest liar who ever lived. I am tempted. My body is tempted to do and desire things that are not right, just like yours. I have the same sensory mechanisms located in my body that you have.

What kept me from taking this woman up on her offer, and what continues to keep me from giving in to this kind of temptation, is my sensitivity to the fact that God is always there. God would know — even if I could hide it from people. You can lie to others and you can lie to yourself, but you cannot lie to God. I thank God for this; I do not ever want to lose this sensitivity. It is my best defense against compromising my integrity.

You can be deceived into thinking that, because no human eye sees you, it is all right to do wrong. But I think about how Potiphar's wife tried to seduce Joseph. Day by day, she spoke to him, offering him the opportunity to lie with her. But Joseph did not heed her. Then came the day when she was finally alone with him. No one would have known. This was the real test.

What did Joseph do? He fled and ran outside. Why did he do a dumb thing like that? Joseph was obviously well aware that God was not only watching out for him, but watching him. Someone would know — in fact, the most important One would know. Just knowing that God sees everything you do, and having a desire to be pleasing in His sight, will keep you out of trouble. Right when you think, *It is such a small thing that it really does not matter in the big picture. Besides, everyone does rolling stops.* It is then that you will remember that it does matter, because it matters to God.

In our country, somehow wrong is considered right, just as long as there are enough other people doing it. But not so with God. What is wrong is wrong in His eyes. If you have a heart not to do wrong, He will let you know when you are about to compromise your integrity. You will know — that is, if you want to know. And that knowing is your integrity talking to you.

Most opportunities to compromise your integrity involve little things here and there – or they start this way. Unless you are committed to doing things right before God, it can be so easy to think "It won't hurt anything or anyone, so what does it matter?" Well, Jesus put it like this, **"He who is faithful in what is least is faithful also in much; and he who**

is unjust in what is least is unjust also in much." Once you allow yourself to cross over into compromising your integrity with the little things, you establish a dangerous precedent and eventually a habit that will affect every area of your life.

This is a critical point. When you get accustomed or habituated to violating seemingly small things, like stop signs, then where do you draw the line? And how do you know that you can control it when you need to? Will you be able to stop before it is too late?

This is why you have to realize that God is watching you. Knowing that God sees everything I do keeps me honest. And this has worked not only for me, but with my family. It particularly has helped in regards to my wife and I raising our children. We were diligent to instill in our children the reality that God is always with them. When we were not able to be there to watch them, they still knew that God sees everything they do. And as a result, we never had a bit of trouble with them. We never had to go to the principal's office, to the police department, or to any other authority because our children were acting up. Our girls went to the same public schools as other children. They had to face the same temptations to drink, try drugs and fornicate. But they had the fear (a reverential fear) of God in them, and this kept them from making many foolish mistakes and messing up their lives.

Unfortunately, a lot of people have lost this sensitivity. Or maybe this truth was never instilled in them, so they do not know. This is tragic because the reality that God will never leave you nor forsake you is what can keep you from making some bad decisions that can affect you the rest of your life. If you think about it, you would find that you would not have made many of the mistakes you have if you had only been sensitive to this reality.

Just knowing that God is ever-present and sees everything can help you to make a habit out of doing what is right. Once doing what you know is right becomes automatic, it is much easier to do right when the stakes are higher. Then you can be trusted with much. So God can — and will — promote you. Others will begin to see you as someone who can be trusted and who is able to handle responsibility and the success that comes with it. Factoring God into this equation makes maintaining your standard of integrity a whole lot easier and comes with a big payoff.

Joseph said, "I cannot sin against God." That was the key to his success and that still is what is critical for you today. The kind of integrity that sets you apart from the rest and ensures your ultimate success is that your first allegiance is to God. Joseph let God set his standard — and so can you. Then, just as God honored Joseph, He will honor you.

No Need to Compromise

Because I have always put my commitment to God first and I do what His Word says to do regarding all of my needs and desires, I am in a position where I cannot be bought. If someone withdraws his support for the ministry I pastor because he does not like what I am called to teach, it will not be detrimental. I do not owe anyone anything, so I do not have to be concerned about what people may or may not think of me.

Of course, I want everyone to think the best of me, but I do not lose any sleep over it. This attitude puts me in a position where I cannot be compromised. Unfortunately, the majority of leaders cannot say this because they are dependent upon the people they lead and serve. So, they have to say and do things to get a certain response from people. They have to act a certain way to get their congregation's approval. I don't; I am free from having to play those games.

This is why I am and can be the same way all the time. I do not have to keep up any front, as it were. I am free to be me, and it is such a wonderful feeling that I will not compromise it for money, support, public approval, or even for friendship. It is just not worth it. I would rather go out of business, so to speak, than compromise my integrity and not be my own man.

I am sure you have figured out that I am not going to tell you what you want to hear just to get you to buy my books or contribute money to the ministry that I pastor. In fact, I am sure some of what I have shared has ruffled feathers. That was not my intent, but it is my responsibility to give people the benefit of what I believe God has given me, whether they like it or not. It is only meant for good, even though sometimes the truth can be hard to take. Nevertheless, if no one buys another one of my books or supports the ministry, then I can always find something else to do. I was not always a pastor.

I think God looks for people who will not compromise. I believe that is why I am in the position I am in today. The scripture says that promotion comes from the Lord; I know this is definitely true because there was no way I could ever have conceived of where I am at this point in my life. I know it is not because of anything that I have done, other than doing what the Word of God says to do. Neither can any man claim that they have made me or the ministry of Crenshaw Christian Center the success that it is. God has promoted me — He did it.

The beauty of all of this is that because no man can claim it, no man can take it away. Nor do I have to worry about how to maintain and sustain it because I did not do it in the first place. It is not mine, it is His.

This is why I say that you want God to promote you. When you seek promotion from man, you can end up owing favors to many different people. So, at some point, you are going to have to compromise your integrity and lose your freedom to be you — unless you do not mind losing your position. This works across the board; it is not just limited to leadership.

Before moving on, I want to point out that the concept of integrity has been a central concern in all religions. This is not surprising since integrity is a kind of wholeness, and most of the world's religions teach that God has called us to an undivided life in accordance with divine command. In other words, we are supposed to have a lifestyle that is dictated by the precepts of that particular religion.

For instance, in Islam this notion is evident in their belief that all rules, legal or moral, are guided by the Charia, the divine path that God directs humans to walk. In Judaism, the study of the Torah and the Talmud reveal the rules under which God's people are expected to live. And in Christianity, the Gospel of Matthew records Jesus telling the people that they are to be pure in heart, which implies an undividedness in following God's rule. This calls for no compromise, no deviation. All of these major religions teach the same principle: There is a price to be paid when it comes to the things of God.

Trust

A person of integrity is someone on whom you can count because he has made the quality decision to act with integrity, has established rules, exercises self-control and is truly willing to stand. Therefore, he is consistent and predictable, and this makes him reliable. After all, how can you count on someone when you never know what he is going to do?

I mention this because there is a difference between acting with integrity and being a person of integrity. Anyone can and may act with integrity at any given time. What makes you a person of integrity is your lifestyle. *Integrity* is a quality or state of being — not, as I said before, a one-time shot. So, inherent in this definition is the implication of consistency and predictability. You are not a person of integrity if you are not consistent and predictable, therefore reliable.

Just look at Jesus. He is the ultimate example of integrity. The Bible says He was without sin; this means that He always did what was right. And what was His character like? The Bible says, **Jesus Christ is the same yesterday, today, and forever**.

This tells me that consistency and predictability is a characteristic of integrity. So, a person of integrity will be the same every day – just like Jesus, the Word of God. He will not change from Monday to Tuesday to Wednesday to Thursday to Friday because his integrity causes him to be consistent and predictable.

I know from personal experience that God is a God of integrity. For more than 30 years I have based my entire life on His Word, and He has never let me down. I have never opened my Bible and discovered that He has had second thoughts and changed what He said. Nor have I ever been left wondering, because His Word tells me what I can expect from Him. He has never failed to do what He says in the Bible. I can trust Him because He has always been reliable — consistent and predictable. Which brings me to what I consider to be another benefit of factoring God into the integrity equation.

For me, trust hinges on Integrity. It is the basis, the foundation, the capstone, of trust. Integrity is not so much an ingredient of leadership as it is a product of leadership. In other words, you must have a reputation for integrity in order to be trusted by others. And this has to be earned, which takes time. Trust does not come overnight. The kind of integrity that proves a person's trustworthiness is demonstrated or seen only over time through his consistency and predictability — this is why being consistent and predictable is so very important.

Can I trust you? How do I know you are trustworthy? The answer lies in yet another question: Can God trust you? It is easy to say yes, but what does your track record actually prove? These are legitimate questions because you are your word and your word is you. If your word is not good, you are no good. If I cannot count on your word, I cannot count on you because you can never be separated from your word.

It is a shame that most people take their words lightly; they do not think it is important or even necessary to keep their word or promises. They do not realize that they lose hold of themselves when they do not make it a point to keep their promises. If you give your word and then do not take adequate steps to keep it, you are not trustworthy. When you say you will do something and then do not do it, you show that you are unreliable and not trustworthy.

It is only over time that you learn that you can trust me. After all, you do not know whether I will do what I say unless you let me, and that takes time. The same is true with God. You cannot really know that God is true to His Word unless you take Him at His Word and see for yourself. The least you can do is give God the same consideration by letting Him prove to you that His Word can be trusted.

What is awesome to me is that by giving you His Word, God has placed Himself in the position of having to prove Himself to you. He does not just expect you to blindly believe, but has made Himself accountable for being reliable so that you can indeed trust Him. And the way that He first begins to establish this trusting relationship with you is in an area that is dearest to most men's heart — their money. He says in Malachi 3:10 to:

> **Bring all the tithes into the storehouse, that there may be food in My house, And try Me now in this," says the LORD of hosts, "If I will not open for you the windows of heaven and pour out for you**

**such blessing that there will not be room enough
to receive it.**

God challenges you to test Him to see that He is reliable, that He is consistent and predictable — and it is only in reference to your giving of money that God invites you to try Him. God certainly knew what He was doing, because money is the one thing that man typically seems to have the greatest difficulty in parting with. I guess it is because most people see money as hard to get and keep. They cannot easily turn it loose. God knew that if you got to the place where you could trust someone with your money, you would trust them with anything.

A lot of people say they trust God, but I wonder if they really do. I equate trusting God to flying in an airplane. When you board a commercial jet, you relinquish your control. Once they shut the doors, back the plane out, and it taxis down the runway and lifts into the sky, you are completely at the mercy of the pilot and the equipment. You are forced to trust; you have no other option. You had a choice before you got on the plane, but not any longer.

The same is true with the heavenly Father. You have a choice as to whether you want to trust in the Word of God. You have a choice of whether you want to hop onboard, so to speak, by accepting His salvation through Jesus Christ. But once you board, if you really want to enjoy the fullness of God, you have to trust Him enough to do things according to His Word.

As passengers are totally dependent upon their airplane and its pilot, so you have to become dependent upon God's Word and not be moved or influenced by your circumstances.

Only then will you get to where you want to go — to your Promised Land. This is why I am making such a point about your own word being good and trusting in God's Word. I see too many people, who say they believe and trust God, whose lives are dictated by their circumstances. They have yet to begin to prove God by becoming a tither. So, I have to wonder.

I say all this to say that if you want to see the integrity of God in your life — if you want what God's Word promises — you have to exhibit integrity yourself. "It takes one to know one," as the old saying goes. You will reap what you sow, but you have to do some sowing first. And the thing is, once you learn to trust God and prove yourself trustworthy in His sight, others can and will trust you.

It all starts with consistency and predictability, so that you are reliable. Being true to your word. Add to this the Word of God and it becomes just a matter of time before promotion comes your way.

Peace

To me, the greatest benefit of living a life of integrity is the peace that comes with it. Isaiah 26:3 declares:

You [the Lord God] **will keep him in perfect peace, whose mind is stayed on You, because he trusts in You.**

I can personally attest to this. I never have wasted half the night tossing and turning because I am worried about the repercussions of something I have done or failed to do. I am fast asleep just as soon as my head hits the pillow.

I am also free to be me. As I have already said, no man is responsible for my success. So I owe no man anything, except the love of Christ. Because I have done things God's way, I do not have any tainted rewards. Sometimes you can get things or have things given to you that turn out to be more trouble than they are worth. You even have cases where, after a person gives you something, he changes his mind and wants it back — especially if you have a falling out. But the blessings of God add no sorrow.

Everything that I have received from the Lord has added to my life. I do not even have to be concerned how I am going to afford the upkeep on the things He has given me because He always sees to it that I have the resources that I need to do so. Nor do I have to be concerned about someone trying to take it. God does not give you something and then take it back. So what I have is mine. There is no downside to any of the many blessings I regularly receive because they are my just reward from my heavenly Father for a job well done. They are rightfully mine to enjoy. Life is really good when you do not have to constantly watch your back and live in fear that something you have done will catch up to you.

You can have this same peace for yourself. But there is a requirement. You first have to do your part. Isaiah 26:3 says that the Lord God will keep him in perfect peace whose mind is stayed on Him — not whose mind is off on a trip somewhere. You have to keep your mind on Him. This does not mean that you go around all day with a picture of God in your head. To have your mind on your heavenly Father is to have your mind on His Word; in other words, to be submitted to (consider and obey) God's Word in all that you do. In plain English, to live by what God's Word says.

The three Hebrew boys were submitted to God in everything. When the decree was passed ordering that the people bow down and worship the image that King Nebuchadnezzar had made, they remained true to the One True God and to the commandment that they have no other gods. They were submitted to the Word of God, rather than the word of man. They went so far as to tell the king that they did not have to answer to him in this matter. Why? Because their conduct — their very lives — were dependent upon the Lord and what His Word says, not upon their circumstances or the price they would have to pay for doing what was right in His sight. God's Word is what dictated the terms of their lives.

Likewise, all day long you have opportunities to make decisions. Keeping your mind stayed on Him means allowing God's Word to be the judge or standard that you use in determining how you will do things and conduct yourself. This means that you have to spend time studying and getting to know what the Bible says so that you can know how to act, what to say, and what your attitude should be in any given situation. This may seem like a lot to do, but it is a small price to pay for such a big reward – not just peace, but the promise of perfect peace. This is the ultimate.

Good Self-Esteem and Confidence

Real confidence and good self-esteem come from integrity based upon the Word of God.

All my life, I had been told to get back because I am black. As a result, I was ashamed of who I was. But one day I got ahold of God's Word, learned about faith (acting on God's Word) and found out that God does not lie. I discovered that through the Bible, God is speaking to me. So I took the Bible personally and literally. And to this day, I remain convinced that the Bible is God talking to me.

I realized that if God says I am something, then it must be true — whether I look like it, feel like it, or even sound like it. Regardless, I still must be that because the Bible says that God cannot lie. And if God cannot lie, then the only alternative is that He must be telling the truth. So, I had to begin to see myself through God's eyes and, consequently, talk the way I see in the Bible that God talks.

At first, my wife and family thought I had gone crazy because I had literally changed overnight. What I mean is that my attitude changed, even though my circumstances were still the same. But I did not let my circumstances discourage me. I was taking God at His Word, so I knew it had to be only a matter of time before my circumstances changed. This is why I do not have much patience for people that tell me they are having such a hard time. They are not having a hard time; it is just a matter of making a decision. They can change in an instant; it does not take six months or five years.

As I mentioned, my circumstances did not change overnight and neither did the way I felt inside. When I first began telling myself "You're more than a conqueror," as it says in the Bible, I would look around to see if anyone was listening because all my life I had been conquered. Slowly but surely, I began to take on the conqueror mentality. I began to talk conqueror talk, began to think conqueror thoughts. Once I did that, I began to see the world in a new light. The same world — nothing had changed, my circumstances were still the same, but I had changed. And when I changed, this change began to exert an influence on my circumstances. Gradually my circumstances began to change for the better as well.

But my change started with a simple decision. I was tired of being defeated, tired of being put down. And so I looked to what God says about me, rather than what people and my circumstances had to say about me. I began to look at my covenant to find out all the things God said about who I am. And, as a result, I became confident.

I have seen in God's Word that I am supposed to think highly of myself. All I have to do is not think more highly than I ought to. Obviously I must be in control of this, or God would not tell me to do something He knows I am incapable of doing. So I did this and it changed me. I just believed God's Word — and if you cannot rely on God's Word, then what can you rely on? If you cannot trust God, who can you trust?

True confidence is a byproduct of a strong relationship with the heavenly Father through His Son, Jesus. You must have a personal relationship with the Father God based upon His Word, the Bible. You must believe and know all that God says about you – not just in terms of what you may have heard or read, but from having lived it out and experienced it.

When you have your relationship with God in the right order, it does not matter what people think. I am at the point now where God's Word is more substantial to me than anyone's opinion. So I trust God that when I do what He tells me to do, people will understand. If not, that is just too bad. I cannot afford to lose any sleep over it because that is what had me down before — going by what people said about me.

You always hear about peer pressure, but that is a bunch of junk. There is no such thing as peer pressure. It is foolish to let some human be your standard instead of God's Word. Do not let other people determine how you see yourself.

Here is how you can know if you are a victim of low self-esteem: It will not be enough for you to accept what God thinks about you. You still have to try to prove yourself to other people. You find yourself in a vicious cycle of constantly trying to please people. But if you see yourself the way God sees you, guess how much sleep you will lose over it?

The Ultimate Guarantee

Living a life of integrity will work to your best interest, especially when it is done for the glory of God. Acting with integrity out of respect for God and His way of doing things gives you a guarantee like none other, and this guarantee is that circumstances will inevitably work to your benefit and all your needs will be covered in the meantime.

In Matthew 6:31-33, Jesus promises:

> **"Therefore do not worry, saying, 'What shall we eat?' or 'What shall we drink?' or 'What shall we wear?'**

"For after all these things the Gentiles seek. For your heavenly Father knows that you need all these things.

"But seek first the kingdom of God and His righteousness, and all these things shall be added to you."

Jesus says not to worry about the necessities of life, for if you are committed to seeking God and doing things His way, this life of integrity ensures that your needs will be met.

Acts 10:34 says:

Then Peter opened his mouth and said: "In truth I perceive that God shows no partiality."

And 1 Samuel 15:29 declares that:

"And also the Strength of Israel will not lie nor relent. For He is not a man, that He should relent."

Since God is no respecter of persons and He does not change His mind or go back on His Word, God is obligated to do for you what He did for Joseph, the three Hebrew boys and Daniel. Joseph says in Genesis 50:20, that **"...You meant evil against me; but God meant it for good,"** and this principle, this blessed assurance is yours as long as you remain committed to living a lifestyle of integrity out of reverence to Him.

If you want this assurance in your life so that your integrity brings you safety, peace, self-esteem and confidence, then the first step is to accept Jesus Christ as your personal

Savior and Lord. You can do this right now and take the first step to living a godly life of integrity by praying this simple prayer:

> *Dear God:*
>
> *I desire to be a person of integrity and to be pleasing in Your sight. I believe You are a God of Integrity and that Your Word is the guide to the truth and to living a lifestyle of integrity.*
>
> *Therefore, I place my trust and confidence in Your Word that says if I confess Your Son Jesus as my Savior and Lord, and believe in my heart that You raised Him from the dead, I will be saved. I trust Your Word, so I believe Jesus Christ is Your Son, and that You sent Him into the world as Savior to redeem my life. I believe He died for me, and that He was raised from the dead. I accept the salvation You have provided for me through Jesus.*
>
> *Jesus, be the Lord over my life. Teach me how to be a person of integrity. I give my life to You and look to You for direction and guidance.*
>
> > *In Jesus' name,*
> > *Amen.*

Whether you prayed this prayer or not, I encourage you to do as the psalmist wrote, **Taste and see that the Lord is good.** What do you possibly have to lose? You will never know that integrity will work to your advantage until you

131

test it out for yourself by making use of the insights I have just shared with you. You simply have too much to lose by leaving this issue to speculation.

For a complete list of books and tapes
by Frederick K.C. Price,
please write to:

Frederick K.C. Price, D.D.
PO Box 90000
Los Angeles, CA 90009

Or visit his website at:
www.faithdome.org

BOOKS BY
FREDERICK K.C. PRICE, D.D.

HIGHER FINANCE
How to Live Debt-Free

RACE, RELIGION & RACISM, VOLUME 1
A Bold Encounter With Division in the Church

THE TRUTH ABOUT ... THE BIBLE

THE TRUTH ABOUT ... DEATH

THE TRUTH ABOUT ... DISASTERS

THE TRUTH ABOUT ... FATE

THE TRUTH ABOUT ... FEAR

THE TRUTH ABOUT ... HOMOSEXUALITY

THE TRUTH ABOUT ... RACE

THE TRUTH ABOUT ... WORRY

LIVING IN HOSTILE TERRITORY
A Survival Guide for the Overcoming Christian

DR. PRICE'S GOLDEN NUGGETS
A Treasury of Wisdom for Both Ministers and Laypeople

BUILDING ON A FIRM FOUNDATION

135

FIVE LITTLE FOXES OF FAITH

THE HOLY SPIRIT:
THE HELPER WE ALL NEED

THE CHRISTIAN FAMILY:
Practical Insight for Family Living
(formerly *MARRIAGE AND THE FAMILY*)

IDENTIFIED WITH CHRIST:
A Complete Cycle From Defeat to Victory

THE CHASTENING OF THE LORD

TESTING THE SPIRITS

BEWARE! THE LIES OF SATAN

THE WAY, THE WALK,
AND THE WARFARE OF THE BELIEVER
(A Verse-by-Verse Study on the Book of Ephesians)

THREE KEYS TO POSITIVE CONFESSION

THE PROMISED LAND
(A New Era for the Body of Christ)

A NEW LAW FOR A NEW PEOPLE

THE VICTORIOUS, OVERCOMING LIFE
(A Verse-by-Verse Study on the Book of Colossians)

NAME IT AND CLAIM IT!
The Power of Positive Confession

ABOUT THE AUTHOR

Dr. Frederick K.C. Price is a world-renowned teacher of the biblical principles of faith, healing, prosperity, and the Holy Spirit. Throughout his more than 45 years in Ministry, countless lives have been changed throughout the world by his dynamic and insightful teaching that truly tells it like it is.

His television program, *Ever Increasing Faith*, has been broadcast throughout the world for more than 20 years and airs in 15 of the 20 largest markets in America, reaching an audience of more than 15 million households each week. His radio program is heard on radio stations across the world, including the continent of Europe via short-wave.

Author of more than 40 popular books teaching practical application of biblical principles, Dr. Price is also the founder and pastor of one of America's largest church congregations, with a membership of more than 18,000. The church sanctuary, the FaithDome, is among the most notable and largest in the nation, with a seating capacity of more than 10,000.

In 1990, Dr. Price founded the Fellowship of Inner City Word of Faith Ministries (FICWFM) that is comprised of more than 300 ministries throughout the world.

Dr. Price holds an honorary Doctorate of Divinity degree from Oral Roberts University, and a honorary diploma from Rhema Bible Training Center.

Dr. Frederick K.C. Price is a 1998 recipient of the Horatio Alger Award. Each year, this prestigious honor is bestowed upon ten "outstanding Americans who exemplify inspirational success, triumph over adversity, and an uncommon commitment to helping others...." Dr. Price also received the 1998 Southern Christian Leadership Conference's Kelly Miller Smith Interfaith Award. This award is given to clergy who have made the most significant contribution through religious expression affecting the nation and the world.

Notes

Notes

Notes

Notes

when you question what
god has done to you, that is
when you are holding something
against God,